A Human Eye

ALSO BY ADRIENNE RICH

Telephone Ringing in the Labyrinth: Poems 2004–2006

Poetry & Commitment: An Essay

The School Among the Ruins: Poems 2000–2004

What Is Found There: Notebooks on Poetry and Politics

The Fact of a Doorframe: Poems 1950–2000

Fox: Poems 1998–2000

Arts of the Possible: Essays and Conversations

Midnight Salvage: Poems 1995–1998

Dark Fields of the Republic: Poems 1991–1995

Collected Early Poems 1950–1970

An Atlas of the Difficult World: Poems 1988–1991

Time's Power: Poems 1985–1988

Blood, Bread, and Poetry: Selected Prose 1979–1985

Your Native Land, Your Life: Poems

Sources

A Wild Patience Has Taken Me This Far: Poems 1978–1981

On Lies, Secrets, and Silence: Selected Prose, 1966–1978

The Dream of a Common Language: Poems 1974–1977

Twenty-one Love Poems

Of Woman Born: Motherhood as Experience and Institution

Poems: Selected and New, 1950–1974

Diving into the Wreck: Poems 1971–1972

The Will to Change: Poems 1968–1970

Leaflets: Poems 1965–1968

Necessities of Life

Snapshots of a Daughter-in-Law: Poems 1954–1962

The Diamond Cutters and Other Poems

A Change of World

A Human Eye

Essays on Art in Society 1997–2008

Adrienne Rich

W. W. NORTON & COMPANY
NEW YORK • LONDON

Printed in the United States of America
First Edition

For information about permission to reproduce selections from this book, write to Permissions, W. W. Norton & Company, Inc., 500 Fifth Avenue, New York, NY 10110

For information about special discounts for bulk purchases, please contact W. W. Norton Special Sales at specialsales@wwnorton.com or 800-233-4830

Manufacturing by Courier Westford
Book design by Chris Welch
Production manager: Devon Zahn

Library of Congress Cataloging-in-Publication Data

Rich, Adrienne Cecile.
A human eye : essays on art in society, 1996–2008 / Adrienne Rich. — 1st ed.
p. cm.
Includes bibliographical references and index.
ISBN 978-0-393-07006-4
1. Poetry—History and criticism. 2. Art and society.
3. Social change in literature. I. Title.

PS3535.I233H86 2009
814'.54—dc22
2008049972

W. W. Norton & Company, Inc., 500 Fifth Avenue, New York, N.Y. 10110
www.wwnorton.com

W. W. Norton & Company Ltd., Castle House, 75/76 Wells Street, London W1T 3QT

1 2 3 4 5 6 7 8 9 0

Contents

Foreword

I AM GRATEFUL to those who instigated some of these essays or made a place for others: Mercury House; Poetry International Web <http://international.poetryinternational.org>; Steve Wasserman, former editor of the *Los Angeles Times Book Review;* Tony Kushner and Alisa Solomon, editors of the anthology *Wrestling with Zion;* the late Alexander Taylor at Curbstone Press; the literary estate of June Jordan and Copper Canyon Press; Ted Genoways at the *Virginia Quarterly Review;* Ocean Press (Australia); Geoffrey O'Brien at the Library of America; University of Stirling in Scotland; the Center for Lesbian and Gay/Queer Studies at the City University of New York; the *Boston Review*; and Jill Bialosky and her colleagues at W. W. Norton & Company for publishing the pocket edition of the lecture "Poetry and Commitment," here reprinted as "Poetry and the Forgotten Future."

As for the poets, thinkers, writers whose words I've dwelt on here, my debt is of course incalculable. I hope this collection may draw other readers to writing that has cleansed the air for me in badly smogged times. Gathering the essays for this volume, I've recognized that together they describe a wider arc: not simply one reader's preferences and choices but an ardent conversation among the quick and the dead, different generations, histories, temperaments.

I've written here mostly about poetry, as it moves through human lives: one activity among many, the art I know best from inside. Throughout I pursue questions of art and political transformation, questions already broached by others, especially in socialist traditions but, in current monologues of marketing and mediocrity, derided or shrugged off along with the socialist vision itself.

Karl Marx—humanist philosopher and social psychologist that he was—described how in the compulsive expansion of capital human senses become starved, reduced to the mere sense of ownership: "an object is only ours when we have it, when it exists for us as capital, or when it is directly eaten, drunk, worn, inhabited . . . *utilized* in some way."

He also observed: "The eye has become a *human* eye only when its object has become a *human*, social object." When art—as language, music, or in palpable, physically present silence—can induce that kind of seeing, holding, and responding, it can restore us to our senses.

And what apprehension, what responsibility then?

Adrienne Rich
2008

A
Human
Eye

Thomas Avena's *Dream of Order*

Sometime in the 1990s the mail brought a literary magazine entitled *The Bastard Review*, with a letter from its editor, Thomas Avena, asking for poems. The quality and range of poetics interested me, as the promised method of payment appealed to me: a package of smoked salmon to be shipped from San Francisco. I sent poems, and the smoked salmon duly arrived. In the same issue was a poem addressed to Alan Turing, the gay British mathematician who cracked the Nazi Enigma code during World War II, later to be convicted of "Gross Indecency," committing suicide two years later. What struck me in the poem was the poise within its tension, the intimate tenderness of the speaker's voice. This was to become the opening poem of Avena's *Dream of Order* (1997), for which I wrote the foreword that follows (in slightly revised form.)

Avena was an artist, an activist, and editor of the anthology *Life Sentences: Writers, Artists, and AIDS* (San Francisco: Mercury House, 1994). He also curated the Smithsonian AIDS history project Face to Face. Living with lymphoma and with many beloved seropositive comrades, Avena was determined to make explicit, investigate,

Preface to Thomas Avena, *Dream of Order* (San Francisco: Mercury House, 1997).

and articulate life and art in the face of debilitating illness and treatments, not to mention official denial. He died at forty-six in 2005, leaving a still-unpublished second book of poetry, *Magi*, and an unfinished expansion of "Marinol," his personal essay in *Life Sentences*.

We became friends, though we met rarely; once, he and his then lover, William Lyon Strong, cooked me a superb dinner in their small apartment (Strong later died of AIDS). We read together at a book festival in San Francisco but mostly exchanged letters and work. He wrote in *Life Sentences* of the heroic effort to go on making art from the truths revealed by disaster, "the divestiture of the body and the implications of such loss for the struggle to create." He was engaged in that effort to the end.

Wherever I turn these days, I'm looking, as from the corner of my eye, for a certain kind of poetry whose balance of dread and beauty is equal to the chaotic negations that pursue us. Amid profiteering language, commoditizing of intimate emotions, and public misery, I want poems that embody—make into flesh—another principle. A complex, dialogic, coherent poetry to dissolve both complacency and despair.

Among the human disasters of the twentieth century, AIDS has summoned up its share of poetry; and under the gaze of AIDS, remarkable poems have been, are being, written. The poems in Thomas Avena's *Dream of Order* are passionately wrought as to craft, tensile, sensual, and delicate, un-selfish in a profound way. For Avena, AIDS is not simply his experience or that of those he has known and loved, concrete as these are in the poems. The plague becomes part of a moral question haunting the generations, specific to now, yet floating in time. Thus poems on the post-Hiroshima architecture of Osaka ("The Rage of Tadao Ando") or Eva Hesse's Holocaust witness in sculpture ("Sans II") along with "5 MOMA Poems in Time of Plague" reiterate art's critical resilience wherever human extremity seems to have crushed all response. Avena implies that art is the projection of that in us which does go on responding, and also that to which our sealed consciousness opens in response.

Most poems "about" visual art tend toward predictable set pieces, appreciations. Film, architecture, pieces of sculpture, painting appear in Avena's work not to be described or commented on but rather invoked, interrogated.

Step back and see it glow
like amber

as if a great wall of scrolls
were touched by burnt
rain;

unreadable
even the shallows

—"Sans II"

He reminds us that not only do we look at extremity through art, we also look at art through extremity's pocked, stained lenses. This is the only "test of time" I can imagine for us who, as Hans Magnus Enzensberger has suggested, are admitted to the bloody "state secrets" of history as voyeurs of mass media, whether accomplices or victims or both.

Avena's technical resources are strong and elastic enough to sustain what he asks his poems to do: ultimately, to mediate between the afflicted and the not-yet-sick, the living, the dying, and the dead. He is inventively expressive: in the twenty-three-space columns of "In a Glass Cage"; in "and who will excavate rooms for the dead?" the notes are a companion prose-poem floating at the end of the poem in verse. Avena's craft doesn't soothe or reassure; it keeps producing tension in the poem, tension in the reader. Poems in very short, broken lines can become tedious; Avena knows and wrestles with the line break, the breath, the inevitable/unexpected.

There are poems here of sexual loss, not through death only but in the after-coital separateness of being and the strictures of self-protection imposed by plague and pregnability, which are not only physical:

What we want
as we wander

the bitter
labyrinth

is the invisible wall;
wall that shields us

from semen
and blood

from the bright seeping
of the vaginal

coil, from
the body's slow rupture

We still crave the body
but we need

its avoidance

and what we want
is impossible

—"Three Men Walking—Giacometti"

Readers from many climates, neighborhoods, predicaments will find Avena's work compelling, disturbing, and confirming. Like the eye of a hurricane, there is a huge calm here in the heart of terribleness. For me, that calm has something to do with integrity of voice. Integrity is hard to isolate or measure except in negatives: the absence of posturing, manipulating, claiming what isn't earned. Integrity saturates the texture of these poems.

Iraqi Poetry Today

Ah! This is Baghdad: I move through it every day, to and fro,
While I squat in this cold exile. I look for it
In the demonstrators who move along Rashid Street carrying banners,
In the strikes of textile workers,
To whom we throw bags of bread and political tracts.
At dawn, carrying paint, we spray the walls with our slogans:
"Down with Dictatorship!"
In the coffee-houses extending along the river on Abu Nawwas,
In the fishermen by the bridge,
In the monument of Jawad Selim which is riddled with bullets,
In Majid's coffeehouse, where the geniuses and informers sip tea,
Where a poet expelled from college gazes at a window
Behind which three Palestinian girls gaze down the street forever.

Review of *Iraqi Poetry Today,* Modern Poetry in Translation, n.s. no. 19, guest ed. Saadi A. Simawe, Kurdish ed. Muhamad Tawfiq Ali, series ed. Daniel Weissbort (London: King's College, 2003). This essay appeared online at Poetry International Web, <http://international.poetryinternational.org>.

Ah! Every morning the war gets up from sleep.
So I place it in a poem, make the poem into a boat, which I throw into the Tigris.

This is war, then.

—from Fadhil al-Azzawi, "Every Morning the War Gets Up from Sleep"

As an American poet, I see my country represented in Iraq by an inept and cruel military occupation, and by a government whose cultural insensibility, at home and abroad, is absolute. Given the first Gulf War, twelve years of disabling sanctions against the Iraqi people, the coup of the 2000 American election, requiring only the 2001 terrorist assaults on home soil to complete consolidation of power into the grasp of the rich and bloody-minded—I begin this review in anger and bitterness, but with profound gratitude for the project, *Iraqi Poetry Today*.

My life would be unthinkable without poetic translation—my own limited efforts to learn from and work with poems in French, Dutch, Italian, Russian, Yiddish, Urdu, Spanish, assisted by dictionaries, literal translations, native linguists, other poets' versions, and the ancient and durable tradition itself. We translate for infusions from poetries we're able to read, and seek out or collaborate on translations from those we cannot read, for illumination of the poetic core of literatures we could not enter any other way. And for other reasons, too, having to do with what in poetry is inimitable, intransigent, telegraphic, musical, explicit, indirect, physical, impalpable, unmistakably human as the human face yet varied as faces are.

To carry the intrinsic nature of a poem from one language to another can mean to make another poem; unweave strands into a new texture; experience the expressive limits of one's mother tongue; make love with a new person, in a different body; work with an unfamiliar medium—to feel the material contradictions of art. In a volume with many co-translators, there is bound to be a mixture of strategies, ranging from the most literal to the most inventive ends of the spectrum.

Poetry from the Arab world was first opened up for me by Salma Khadra Jayyusi's magnificent *Modern Arabic Poetry: An Anthology* (New York: Columbia University Press, 1987), in which she rightly says that since there can be no "perfect equivalence" in the translation of poetry, "the task of translating [is] not only a major aesthetic undertaking but also a crucial social responsibility." Subjective, emotional experience everywhere lives and converses in poetry. Yet subjective emotions exist of necessity in dialogue with objective conditions. Poetry springs from a nexus of individual and shared experience, above all an experience of *location*—geophysical realities, visible landscape, spaces marked out by religion, education and politics, poverty and wealth, gender and physiognomy, subordination and independence. Poetry both articulates new upshootings of particularity and grows out of a traditional compost. And it is often written in a desire to change the composition of the very soil from which it grows.

In his introduction to *Iraqi Poetry Today,* Saadi A. Simawe admits to a disappointed hope for his undertaking: that "translating poetry might contribute to the appreciation of other civilizations and even to peace in the Middle East. It seems [in the light of September 11, 2001] that our dream has failed." I want to urge him not to abandon hope. Conflicts waged by political/economic powers may be carried on light-years behind immense transformations in public consciousness. In the twenty-first century, war is an anachronism maintained through advanced technology and manipulated emotions, on behalf of corporate power, in the name of chauvinism. Yet old notions of heroism and glory, still pushed by the war makers, are fraying. An enormous international revulsion against war showed its face in mass demonstration upon mass demonstration during the months before Bush, Cheney, and Rumsfeld invaded Iraq. That revulsion has been a presence in poetry for centuries.

Simawe goes on to say: "The globalization of capital threatens to extinguish the spirit of each culture, but one positive change has come with this movement. It has shed light on the importance of translation. Translation can, of course, be seen as a tool that facilitates the globalization of capital and thus contributes to the overall deadening of cultures, but when poetry is translated, it works against these effects." I agree in principle but would argue with the generalization. A poem is indeed something different from advertising copy or a best-selling novel or computer manual or mass-circulation magazine. Yet whose poetry is translated, from and into which languages, what of the poetry actually translated can get published and receive international distribution, what poets (and what poetics) are disseminated, and who decides these matters—such questions vibrate beneath Simawe's claim. The corporatization of publishing and book distribution, the funding sources for cultural journals, the class and gender relations that create an international literary/intellectual elite, all come into play here. (Of the forty poets in this anthology, just four are women, one of whom, Sajidah al-Musawi, is described as "an Iraqi woman poet, writing in Arabic. No further information about her is available." I can't but wonder why. One, Nazik al-Mala'ika, now living in Egypt, is considered "the most important woman poet and critic in the Arab world." With Badr Shakir al-Sayyab, according to Salma Jayyusi, she liberated Arab poetry from formalism. Of the thirty-odd translators, incidentally, fifteen are women.)

Reviewing a book-length poem by Egyptian poet Muhammad Afifi Matar, Saadi Simawe and Carolina Hotchandani note "how influential English translation has recently become on the literary standard in the Arab world. Whether or not a piece of literature is translated into English practically determines the artistic value of that work. At this early stage of globalization it is difficult to determine whether this phenomenon is enriching Arabic literary tradition."

In his introduction to *Iraqi Poetry Today,* Simawe observes that "whether we like it or not, English has become the world language, and thus has come to belong to people of all nations. Hundreds of the poets who live in exile have lost their audience and have begun to write either in English or to get their poetry translated into English or the language of their host country. The outcome of this hybrid poetics has become an important feature of western modernism." So, Western poetry is enhanced. At the same time, "major critics in the

West are not familiar with, and some not even interested in, the languages of the colonized." Indeed. And a Western reader like myself may approach an anthology like this sketchily versed, or not at all, in the literary contexts and traditions behind the making of the poems.

Clearly reflected, however, are politically repressive conditions such as those within Iraq under the dictatorship, and the Iran–Iraq War, which sent most of the poets in this book into exile. Five of the forty still live in Iraq; the majority are scattered in Damascus, London, Germany, California, Denmark, Geneva, Egypt, Detroit, Israel, Cambridge (Massachusetts), Tripoli, Sweden; some, like Abd al-Wahhab al-Bayyati and S'adi Yusuf, having moved for a lifetime "from exile to exile." Most of them have been identified with the Left and have paid the price. The loss, to any country, of its creative and rebel spirits is more than just a "brain drain." These are the damages wreaked by brutalities from within. (The deaths of more than 300,000 Iraqi children alone from acute malnutrition, first as a result of economic sanctions, the mortality rate rising after the U.S. and British invasion in March [2003], represent an incalculable national loss inflicted by brutalities from without.)

Standard Arabic, Hebrew, Iraqi dialect, and Iraqi Kurdish are the languages of these poets. The Kurdish editor, Muhamad Tawfiq Ali, suggests the internal tensions of an ethnic minority poetry in a brief, somewhat ironic essay centering on Goran and Bekes, pseudonyms of the father figures of Kurdish modernism. "The stark irony," Ali tells us, "is that the proletarian poet [Goran] wrote in the social dialect of the bourgeoisie, whereas the nationalist [Bekes] wrote in the dialect of the working class and peasants. . . . Goran's poetry is formal, indirect and subtle: Bekes is informal, direct and popular or simple." I wish that Ali had said more about the politics of Kurdish nationalism (and internationalism), from which these and later Kurdish poets such as Bulland al-Haydari emerged. The relationship of nationalism and language (or vernacular) is of special interest where poetry is concerned, as cultural resistance to ethnic or colonial domination.

I have found myself, by default, reading these translations more for images and themes than for their verbal quality. In part this has, obviously, to do with my own outsider relation to the languages they were written in and the traditions they represent. But the versions also seem uneven: many feel to me at one or two stages of craft behind the level of poetic rendering that Khaled Mattawa, for example, Libyan American and himself a fine poet in English, has given to the poems of S'adi Yusuf, both here and in the recently published collection *Without an Alphabet, without a Face: Selected Poems of Saadi Youssef* (St. Paul, Minn.: Greywolf Press, 2002) or of many poems in Jayyusi's *Modern Arabic Poetry: An Anthology* or Nathalie Handal's *The Poetry of Arab Women: A Contemporary Anthology* (New York: Interlink, 2001). There are phrasings that trouble me, as in Fawzi Karim's "What Was My Choice?":

I

One has learned to allow a tiny space in the head for contingency.

Yet, losses befall suddenly
—of the river and the date palms that used to balance
of the friends circling your glass like a crescent.

Then you in one moment peel yourself of whom you love
and alone, dim-sighted, grope your way home,
the light of the street lamps heavier than darkness
the burden of exile than in memory.

Tantalizing ourselves with hope
shielding ourselves against . . . but the question in the
 middle of exiles suddenly attacks:
—What have you chosen?

No longer trusting ourselves
about to desert the self,
annihilated in God's self,
or prefer to watch, like a trap,
the tripwires of another.

—April 10, 2000

II

When exile took us by surprise,
a surgeon ready-scrubbed
he treated us with scalpels
cleansed us of the dream tumours in our organs,
and pushed us into the last scene of the shadow theatre
in order that we perform for him our secondary roles

Who are we? Fury of a blind man
being led by a thread of loss,
dice thrown on the night's page
without even an echo of their
rolling.

—April 11, 2002

In an affecting and immediate poem, with memorable images such as the "friends circling your glass like a crescent," exile as surgical excision, the rolling of soundless dice, the lapses into awkward English syntax are especially jarring. Phrases like "peel yourself of whom you love," "the burden of exile than in memory," "the question in the middle / of exiles" (at the core of exile?), "prefer to watch, like a trap" (preferring?), "the tripwires of another" (another's tripwires?"), "in order that we perform for him" (to perform for him?) seem to need more attention to values of the ear. Similarly, in two poems by Abd al-Karim Kassid, the word "stature" is used where "body" or "figure" is meant; *stature* refers only to height or dimension, but an entire corpus is implied here: "The tree is a stature / and the leaf, an eye."

To transfer the tonalities of Arabic (in which most of the poems were written) into English would be, I assume, a challenging task, akin to rendering the music of Spanish or Russian. Sometimes a single word seems ill-chosen, particularly when repeated over and over, as "calamity" in Murad Mikha'il's long, accumulative poem "You Have Your Calamity and I Have Mine." The word "calamity" is rather weak syllabically to bear the weight of many repetitions: why not "disaster"? Mikha'il is an Iraqi Jew and seems to address an Arab world of which he both is and is not a part. The poem is extraordinarily interesting, but "calamity" sounds almost Victorian in the face of what it's evoking.

As I've gone deeper into this collection, the flaws have seemed almost negligible beside what I've carried away from the whole ("almost" because each word in each poem/translation does matter). There is the remarkable transcription of Mazaffar al-Nawwab reciting his long poem "Bridge of Old Wonders" for a live audience. Al-Nawwab, described as "the most popular poet in the Arab world," is a performance poet whose works circulate almost entirely through pirated cassettes. The poem moves from invocation through rich and allusive imagery into symbolic narrative, from delicacy to machismo, from a "high" poetic tone to colloquialism and dialogue, from Iraqi cities to a Palestinian refugee camp, from mourning to scathing invective, whose objects range from oil sheikhs to the "Arabs of silence" to Yasīr 'Arafāt to Henry Kissinger. For all its declamatory intensity, it's highly layered and textured, requiring the many notes provided for the Anglophone reader, as if T. S. Eliot and Amiri Baraka had spent a long night together.

Finally, Iraq's great innovative woman poet Nazik al-Mala'ika, represented here by ten pages of poetry. "Jamilah and us" addresses the moral problematics of protest poetry—in this case, the many poems written on the imprisonment and torture by the French of a young Algerian resistance fighter: **"The details of your torture were on every tongue, / And that hurt us, it was hard for our sensitive ears to bear / . . . Did we not use her suffering to give meaning**

to our poetry? / Was that a time for songs?" Her longer poems here suggest an impressive authority of voice that in the English doesn't quite carry over; the invocative "To Poetry" is marred by phrases like "raving fragrance," "heaving with yearning." The largeness of her scope and vision are most apparent in the mystical-political "The Hijrah [Migration] to God," which begins as an ecstatic praise song and ends

O my king, the journey has lengthened, lengthened,
and ages have passed,
and between locked worlds I have sailed, asking at doors.
I carried with me the wounds of fedayeen,
and the taste of death in September, and of mud.
I carried with me the sorrows of Jerusalem, O my king,
and the wound of Jenin,
and a night of high walls that cannot be scaled.
So where is the door? Where is the door?
My sacrifices are heaped at the altar,
my Quran is hidden in the mist,
and the agony of my Al-Aqsa mosque
cuts me like a knife. . . .

How can we spend the night in captivity?
And how can we sleep, expelled from our homes? . . .
And you stay with the slain, o my king, and with the wounded,
you stay at your post, vigilant.
And here we have lost the religion, and fought our beloved fedayeen.

We spilled blood in Beirut,
we poured blood in Amman,
and with our hands, we made our land a guillotine for our people.

One reads, guessing: Is this or that poem actually more remarkable than translation can suggest? is it, in translation, bound, like Prometheus, on the rock of language and cultural references? Has the translation been timid, binding itself within the literal or within an idea of Anglophone poetic language (e.g., "wondrous"), which, to an American eye and ear, seem artificial? How have twentieth-century movements in Arabic poetry, from traditional to modernist poetics with blendings of both, found correspondence in English? Is it mere chance that the poems by Ronny Someck, born in Baghdad but living most of his life in Israel, seem verbally so fresh and audacious? Yet gathered here, these multi-exiled, strongly identified voices possess an energy for which I can only reaffirm my gratitude.

Translation is a dangerous and indispensable art. Likewise, criticism of translation by one unfamiliar with the original languages must come with many caveats. But a complex and vivid humanity, an aching for freedom resounding throughout this collection, should nourish the hope in which it was conceived and carried through—even as Iraq, its people, its poets still dwell in hunger and under fire.

Jewish Days and Nights

EVERY DAY IN my life is a Jewish day. Muted in my house of origin, Jewishness had a way of pressing up through the fissures. But only in my college-dormitory years did it become a continuous conversation, as Israel was declared a nation-state, Brandeis University founded as the first private university committed to diversity. (The Holocaust went almost unmentioned in those late 1940s–early 1950s of postwar optimism and amnesia.) On an early date I was taken for a walk by an intense young man who talked about Kafka and whose first name was the same as my father's. Too intense, it felt; I had been deciding that at college I would be "normal," not "special."

Jewishness was muted in my house of origin, but the sense of specialness was not: that house was—intensely—different from the homes of my middle-class, non-Jewish friends. For one thing it was full of books. I started off intellectually in my father's eclectic library, which included Maimonides and Dostoyevsky, Spinoza and Carlyle, Dante and Darwin, Edwin Arnold's *The Light of Asia* and Oscar Wilde's poems, Ibsen and William Blake, Heine and Cervantes and

From Tony Kushner and Alisa Solomon, eds., *Wrestling with Zion: Progressive Jewish-American Responses to the Israeli-Palestinian Conflict* (New York: Grove Press, 2003).

Sigrid Undset, a set of Chekhov's stories and a big blue volume of the *Trial of Jeanne d'Arc*. Medical books (he was a pathologist) were on the lowest shelves; books deemed unfit for young eyes stored high up under the ceiling—an unexpurgated edition of the *Thousand and One Nights,* a manual for *Ideal Marriage,* both revelatory (once I was able to get at them) about heterosexual erotics. No Freud, no Marx. Veblen's *Theory of the Leisure Class,* a title that caught my eye but did not hold me. Also Bernard Shaw's *The Intelligent Woman's Guide to Socialism and Capitalism,* but since in my teens I had not yet heard of either system, I passed on that interesting title.

I'm remembering a library I was foraging in between 1938 and 1947, accumulated since my father's youth. So every day in my life even then was, in fact, a Jewish day, little as I thought about it.

Because the freedom of that library—whatever its limitations—let me know that it's possible and necessary to be interested in everything: Hindu mythology, the mud-blotted villages of Chekhov's peasants in Czarist Russia, the sound of an eighteenth-century English poem ("I wander through each charter'd street / Near where the charter'd Thames doth flow") or Bible cadences ("Would God I had died for thee, O Absalom, my son, my son"); and the French Revolution. To assume that philosophy, history, foreign literatures in translation, novels, plays, poetry of many kinds belonged together in one room of the mind. That there are many worlds with many texts worth reading—this included my father's admiration for Arab culture, partly "orientalist" but deeply respectful of its learning, especially its medicine, its architecture, its dignity.

Elsewhere I have described my father as an "assimilated Jew." He was also a Southerner, born in Birmingham, Alabama, to parents (Ashkenazic and Sephardic) who had reason for cautiousness among white Southern Christian neighbors. But I believe that in his mind, for various reasons, every day of his life was a Jewish day. It was also a day of thinking about science, the description of objective phenomena, the relation of disease to its environment—micro and macro. During most of my childhood, for ten years, besides teaching medical students and running a department, he was writing a comprehensive text on tuberculosis. His promotion to full professor was delayed by anti-Semitism (the Johns Hopkins School of Medicine, modeled on the German academic system, had never had a Jewish department chair).

These memoiristic paragraphs are my way of suggesting that a Jewish day can have many dimensions. When I think—daily—about American Jews and Israel, about Zionism and the Middle East, about intellectual and political life in this country and elsewhere, I start from there. A library. An attitude.

The Israeli novelist Shulamith Hareven, born in Europe, has described herself as more Levantine—by disposition and sympathies—than Ashkenazic Israeli:

> **Authentic Levantism means the third eye and the sixth sense. It is the keen sensitivity to "how," the knowledge**

> that "how" is always more important than "what;" therefore every true artist is a kind of Levantine. It means a perpetual reading between the lines, both in human relations and in political pronouncements—an art no Israeli political leader has yet succeeded in acquiring. . . .
>
> Levantism . . . is the tacit knowledge that different nations live at different ages, and that age is culture, and that some nations are still adolescent, among them, quite often, Israel. And it is the bitter experience that knows that everything—every revolution, every ideology—has its human price, and there is always someone to pay it. It is the discerning eye, the precise diagnosis, that sees the latent narcissist in every ideologue. It is the joke at his expense, and the forgiveness.

What Hareven is describing is the dynamic life of what in the United States we woodenly term "multiculturalism," giving it an ideological salute with little sense of how it might be, has been lived, over centuries, not only in the Middle East, along rivers and trade routes, in villages and cities and in the exchange of letters and manuscripts, medicinal herbs and culinary spices, surgical and musical instruments, poetry and dance, food and seeds and attitude.

But this *is* what Jews have lived, sometimes turning outwardly toward it (if perforce in covert resistance—the Marranos), sometimes assuming that an intellectually vibrant dominant culture (Enlightenment Germany) could absorb us harmlessly, sometimes living theocratic, hemmed-in, separatist reductions of Eastern European Judaism (Mea Shearim, Williamsburg). Yet diaspora—a multifaceted condition—means never always, or anywhere, being just like other Jews. It means class and cultural difference, dissension, contradiction, different languages and foods, living in different ages and relationships to tradition, world politics, and the "always/already" of anti-Semitism.

Edmond Jabès:

> "Where do you come from, brother with the white face?"
> "I come from that white part of the world where I was not."
>
> "Where do you come from, brother with the dark skin?"
> "I come from that black part of the world where I was not."
>
> "Where do you come from, brother with the pale face and bent back?"
> "I come from the boundless ghetto where I was born."

Hareven ends her essay,

> I am a Levantine because I see war as the total failure of common sense, an execrable last resort. And because I am a Levantine, all fundamentalists on all sides, from Khomeini to Kahane, will always want to destroy me and all Levantines like me, here and in the neighboring countries.

Beyond the loss of millions of minds in the death camps, I wonder if there has been anything more impoverishing to Jewish ethical and intellectual culture in the second half of the twentieth century than the idea of Jewish sameness, Jewish unanimity, marching under one tribal banner. (Dissidence and argument are part of all human existence, in no way exclusively Jewish. But they have been acutely characteristic of Jewish life, political or religious, socialist or Talmudist: the question that begets a question.) This orthodoxy, relating to Jewishness and Israel, has long prevailed in self-declared mainstream American Jewish circles (centering around synagogues and Jewish philanthropies) and has been received—indeed, in many quarters welcomed—as the official Jewish voice. It has framed such concepts as Zionism; the absolute historical uniqueness of the Final Solution (hideously unique in some ways, in other ways a successor and predecessor of other genocides); or the representative character of European Jewish experience, whether in Western or Eastern Europe (a historical ignorance or marginalizing of Jewish histories and cultures in those parts of the world colonized by Christian Europe.) This Eurocentrism has been absurdly parochial (Hareven notes American-born Golda Meir's horror at the Middle Eastern—Levantine—food she found Israelis eating), racist even toward other Jews, and disastrously blind and deaf to those non-Jews whose fates in suffering were and are linked to Jewish fates (as in "a land without a people for a people without a land"). The history of Zionism itself, within Europe, as a much-debated and debatable strategy has been conveniently submerged. Israel itself, and U.S. military aid to Israel, have until recently been untouchable by controversy or criticism.

Clare Kinberg, a longtime activist for justice within several Jewish communities and a founding editor of the Jewish feminist journal *Bridges,* has told this story:

> **Recently I was speaking with some younger activists about the deep divisions within the Jewish community, and the difficulty of expressing a "peace with justice" agenda within Jewish settings in the U.S. The experience of younger activists is that the last two years of explosive violence in Israel have so terrorized the [U.S.] Jewish community that any sympathy for Palestinian suffering is equated with betrayal. The Jewish community has never been so divided, the young activists told me. My perspective is a bit different.**
>
> **In the early 1980s, at a public meeting with the Israeli consulate at the St. Louis Jewish Community Center, I asked a question based on my reading of former Jerusalem Deputy Mayor Meron Benevisti's "five minutes to midnight" thesis: Do you think Jewish settlement on the West Bank might make it harder for Jews and Palestinians to eventually reach a negotiated agreement? For this question, I was spit on and physically chased from the room.**

Kinberg goes on:

> **Now, twenty years later, my question is mundane. A November 2002 survey of American Jews revealed that 51.7% supported a solution to the conflict on the basis of the Clinton Proposals—two states, evacuation of most settlements, withdrawal to the 1967 border with adjustments, and a shared capital in Jerusalem. . . . Twenty years ago mere mention of ideas such as this landed and branded you outside the community.**

Ignorance—or suppression—of the Jewish tradition of secular heretics and radicals who have repeatedly emerged at the crossroads of culture and thought. An idolatry of certain select aspects of Jewish experience at the expense of others. An American Jewish default toward the Holocaust when politically challenged, a tendency to privilege Jewish suffering over all the sufferings of human history. A pulling away from centuries of Jewish conversation about justice, ethics, human rights, property, our obligations to others, toward Israel-centric chauvinism, fundamentalist ideas of blood and soil. These have been part of the price paid for middle-class Jewish American identity—and for the problematic and controversial "whiteness" of American Jews, the idolatry of class success that has disidentified itself from American class and racial struggles.

That intellectual price reveals itself where neoconservative Jews accept Christian Identity fundamentalists as their "pro-Israel" allies or where Jewish students on university campuses are prompted to treat critiques of Israel and the Occupation, or protests against the unholy alliance between the Bush and Sharon governments as anti-Semitism, pure and simple. Anti-Semitism, crude and subtle, certainly exists on campuses. Universities are not charmed moral spaces. But to reduce every question to anti-Semitism is to become infected with anti-Semitism's toxic spirit. (Not to do so is surely difficult for young Jews raised in the pro-Israel monologue, facing controversy and politics perhaps for the first time. I well remember arguing politics out of my father's mouth, at college, not really wanting to know that there were other arguable positions of which I hadn't a clue.) It is, of course, scalding to be called a "self-hating Jew" because you won't name yourself a Zionist. It's also a psychologizing diagnostic label for a real, historical political position.

The ideas of Jews like Marx and Rosa Luxemburg fired a Jewish generation who were mostly non-Zionist, believing that if social revolution could ignite throughout the world there would be less and less room for anti-Semitism in a socialist international community. Many of that Eastern European generation emigrated to America to vitalize labor, antiracist, and socialist movements in the United States. But even Zionist pioneers, as the Marxist historian Isaac Deutscher points out, were imprinted with revolutionary socialist ideals, which they carried to Palestine: ideas of egalitarian community, of mending the division between mental and manual labor.

Writing in the 1950s and early 1960s of a very new Israel, Deutscher remarks that as a young Marxist he had been anti-Zionist; after the Final Solution he described himself as a "non-Zionist"—a position he would argue with leading Israelis, including David Ben-Gurion and Moshe Sharett. Critical of nationalism, recognizing Zionism's inevitable realization at the end of World War II, he was certainly taken with Israel's energies and contradictions; he felt the utopian, collective, secular attractions of the kibbutz and also saw its role as military outpost: "The bastions of Israel's Utopian socialism bristle with Sten-guns." He did not minimize Israeli danger; his sense of the meaning of Palestinian dispossession and displacement now seems tone-deaf for an internationalist. (As was common in the 1960s, he recognized no Palestinians, only Arabs in general.) He also noted that Israel's economy, only partly because of Arab boycotts, had virtually no base apart from American Jewish donations and U.S. aid.

I first read Isaac Deutscher's *The Non-Jewish Jew* in 1982, a time of newly reminted Left Jewish identity in the United States, and of a Jewish feminism trying to locate itself in multiracial feminist identity politics. Into this burst the massacres in Sabra and Shatila, the first intifada, and a sharpened consciousness of Palestinian presence, history, and politics. I found colleagues and comrades among Jewish activists—feminist, lesbian, gay, communist, socialist, offspring of communists—reckoning with the wasteland bequeathed by Stalinism and McCarthyism, and with the acute tension between the antiracist, anticolonial politics we believed in and the question of

Israel. Let's say those were not easy years. Deutscher's book went past me, as it were; even its title sounded too much like escapism.

Rereading it in the past months, I found it mostly acute, generous, accessible—the essays of a former cheder prodigy from Poland who, intended for a rabbi, turned from religion; got expelled from the Polish Communist Party over the question of international social revolution versus "socialism in one country"; lived in exile; became an anti-Stalinist historian who eloquently made English his fourth or fifth language; wrote respected and lasting biographies of both Stalin and Trotsky; and to the end kept his eye on Jewish complexity and its relationship to the hope of international socialism. In 1954 he wrote of Middle Eastern politics:

> As long as a solution . . . is sought in nationalistic terms both Arab and Jew are condemned to move within a vicious circle of hatred and revenge. . . . In the long run a way out may be found beyond the nation-state, perhaps within the broader framework of a Middle East federation.

Shulamith Hareven's sense of Levantism in political terms.

I've said that "American Jews" have paid an intellectual and spiritual price for the narrowing of sight demanded by conformity and reliance on Israel as surrogate identity. Part of this price has been estrangement of many Jews from any Jewish affiliation. But, of course, in reality American Jews disagree like all other Jews, past and future. I share the hopes of those working to create a specific countervoice to AIPAC and the Conference of Presidents of Major American Jewish Organizations, as the organizers of Brit Tzedek v'Shalom (Jewish Alliance for Justice and Peace) seek to do—an intervention in the monologue. I'm grateful for the multiracial coalition work of Jews for Racial and Economic Justice in New York, and the Los Angeles–based Progressive Jewish Alliance, activists who recognize that American Jews have every reason to oppose, as Jews, the accelerating dismemberment of democracy in and by the United States. And for international groups like Women in Black, Rabbis for Human Rights, and especially Israeli-Palestininan groups like Bat Shalom and Ta'ayush. My days usually begin with reading e-mailed columns from Jewish Voice for Peace, whose critical and balanced editorial comments accompany articles from international sources including *Haaretz* and *Al-Ahram*, the *Jerusalem Post* and the *Electronic Intifada,* as well as periodicals in the United States, Britain, and Europe.

The whiteout of American Jewish dissent is starting to crack like old plaster, even under Bush administration moves to paralyze and penalize dissent. The cynicism of official United States support for an expansionist Israel grows more obvious as American troops (and a preemptive nuclear policy) are being massed against Iraq and as Israeli democracy quivers like a reed. But the mobilization of public antiwar sentiment, from a remarkable spectrum of Americans, including thousands of Jewish activists, is also mounting as I write this.

And the words and actions of Israeli dissidents, including feminists, "refuseniks," and high-school students, groups like New Profile and the Israeli Committee against House Demolitions, have borne courageous, often physically endangered witness to "another Israel."

Israeli Jews are a fractured population, as among European, Levantine, Ethiopian, U.S.-born, Russian, Israeli-born, and newer immigrants, secular and observant, left-wing and right-wing parties, with in-group differences as well. Neither Israeli nor Palestinian society is a seamless, monochrome garment: hope as well as difficulty lies in this recognition. Yet mainstream sources of information in the United States convey only one-dimensional representations of all this internal complexity, and organized American Jewish opinion has yet to become as expressive of political differences and contradictions as the Israeli press has been, even under a military government in a climate of increasing insecurity.

Emeritus Harvard Hillel Rabbi Ben-Zion Gold, describing himself as as a lifelong Zionist, a survivor of the camps, "devoted to Israel," calls on American Jews

> to discover their own focus, independent from Israel . . . to link up with [the] proud history of the Diaspora. They have to rediscover their cultural, religious, and political gravity. . . . At present, the task of Jews who are committed to the welfare of Israel is to hold up the critical mirror for Americans and Israelis . . . a thankless but important task.

> **. . . It is not American Jewish criticism that has created sympathy for the Palestinians. It is the suppression of millions of Palestinians over thirty-five years that has done it. It is a pity that the Israeli government has never expressed regret for the harm it has done to the Palestinians during the occupation. An ounce of compassion would go a long way.**

And perhaps the nineteenth-century word *Zionism*—so incendiary, so drenched in idealism, dissension, ideas of blood and soil, in memories of victimization and pursuant claims of the right to victimize—perhaps the use of this word, by Zionists, post-Zionists, and anti-Zionists alike, needs to dissolve before twenty-first-century realities. Israel's "right to exist" is still questioned and challenged in some quarters. Yet it does exist—buttressed by an unprecedentedly reckless U.S. military-industrial complex—as an expansionist nuclear state, with a thirty-five-year history of military occupation, in a world where the right to exist is endangered for all, some more immediately than others. Israel is no longer, if it ever truly was, a "place where Jews can be safe," in a world where national borders have become so discrepant with actual human migrations and displacements, where religious zealotry and imperial will outpace ethical understanding, and where the urgency of possible extinction is everywhere heavy on the air. A world where Jewish survival is inextricable from the survival of everyman and everywoman. Like the United States, Israeli civil society is permeated with contradictions and social inequities, promises and betrayals, chauvinism and self-interrogation. The citizens of neither state can, in good faith, afford the illusion of exceptionalism.

Would a new focus for American Jews transcend voting for a (Democratic or other) Party hack who happens to be Jewish? Moving beyond myth and monologue, would it become a critique of false loyalties, an argument with power and privilege? A new relation to the "proud history of the Diaspora?"

Somewhere in the close distance someone is asking: : *But—do you love the Jewish people?*

—What do you think I'm doing here?

Isaac Deutscher ended his 1954 essay on "Israel's Spiritual Climate":

> **. . . Sometimes it is only the music of the future to which it is worth listening.**

Every day was a Jewish day for the socialist intellectual who provocatively called us to acknowledge the possibility of a "non-Jewish Jew." Not a Jew trying to pass, deny, or escape from the wounds and fears of the community, but a Jew resistant to dogma, separatism, to "remembering instead of thinking," in Nadine Gordimer's words—anything that shuts down the music of the future. A Jew whose solidarity with the exiled and persecuted is unrestricted. A Jew without borders.

The most thoughtful of my brothers turned to me and said:
"If you make no difference between a Jew and a non-Jew, are you, in fact, still a Jew?"

I began with a Jewish library. As I write these sentences, there's a disc playing—Solomon Burke singing "None of us are free / while one of us is chained." He's not a Jew. But it's a Jewish night. One of my Jewish days and nights.

Muriel Rukeyser for the Twenty-first Century

I have written of Muriel Rukeyser in *What Is Found There: Notebooks on Poetry and Politics* (New York: Norton, 1993) and Jan Heller Levi, ed., *A Muriel Rukeyser Reader* (New York: Norton, 1994). In 2003 Geoffrey O'Brien of the Library of America asked me to edit and introduce a selection of Rukeyser's poetry for the American Poets Project. The essay here, written for that volume, carries my thinking about her across the century's divide. It was no easy task to distill a compact volume from a life work so large in every sense. Now, the 650-page *Collected Poems* (ed. Janet E. Kaufman and Anne F. Herzog with Jan Heller Levi [Pittsburgh: University of Pittsburgh Press, 2005]) stands as the authoritative version of that work.

MURIEL RUKEYSER WAS a major and prolific American poet and writer and, through most of her life, a political and cultural activist. Besides her 650-page *Collected Poems*, she left behind three biographies; a musical play, *Houdini;* a quite unclassifiable, mesmerizing narrative called *The Orgy;* trans-

Preface to Muriel Rukeyser, *Selected Poems,* ed. Adrienne Rich, American Poets Project (New York: Library of America, 2004).

lations from the Mexican poet Octavio Paz and the Swedish poet Gunnar Ekelöf; *The Life of Poetry,* a study of poetics and social crisis; and still uncollected essays, journalism, letters, film scripts, and plays. Her reputation has endured many pendulum swings in her lifetime and beyond; her work has not been easy to assess or appropriate in the ways that many poets can be packaged for consumption. Her breadth of concern with the world was large, her issues and literary techniques many, and she refused to compartmentalize herself or her work, claiming her right to intellect and sexuality, poetry and science, Marxism and myth, activism and motherhood, theory and vision. None of these were scattershot "phases," for she was one of the great integrators, seeing the fragmentary world of modernity not as irretrievably broken, but in need of societal and emotional repair.

Born in 1913 "in the first century of world wars" ("Poem"), Rukeyser grew up in New York City as the elder daughter of secular Jewish parents from Yonkers and Milwaukee, on the cusp of prosperity: her mother a onetime bookkeeper and her father a concrete salesman who became partner in a sand-and-gravel company. The city itself was growing around her by means of hand-thrown fiery rivets, poured cement, huge machines, intensive development. "Each of these apartment houses, standing like dead trunks along the avenue, has its army of children." Around them, "the city rises in its light. Skeletons of buildings; the orange-peel cranes; highways put through; the race of skyscrapers. And you are a part of this."

There were nannies, a chauffeur-driven car, upwardly mobile aspirations. “I was expected to grow up and become a golfer”—a suburban professional’s wife. Books and the arts were regarded as decoration, but good education provided—private schooling, Vassar College for two years. A downturn in the family fortunes after the economic crash of 1929 caused her to leave Vassar and conventional formal education. The girl being readied for successful matronhood was from a young age a reader, an explorer of the city with the children’s gangs in her neighborhood, and a secret writer of poems before she knew there were living poets. (“All are dead; the musicians, the poets, the sculptors. This is a world of business. Real men go to the office.”) And “it was clear to a growing child that the terrible, murderous differences between the ways people lived were being upheld all over the city.”

Muriel Rukeyser was a new kind of American, intensely and for her entire life identified with one city, yet internationalist in her spirit and actions; journeying worldwide yet rooted. Her poetry embraces both New York, which in some poems becomes virtually part of her body, and places whose conflicts and configurations entered her psyche: Gauley Bridge, West Virginia; Catalonia during the Spanish Civil War; the Outer Banks; the Ajanta Caves in India; Ireland; Vietnam; South Korea.

Few American poets have understood as Rukeyser did how the individual life, even if unconscious or apathetic to the fact, is shaped in history and in collectivity. She created a poetics of historical sensibility: not as nostalgia but as resource to express and interpret contemporary experience and imagine a different future.

Organize the full results of that rich past
open the windows : potent catalyst

she wrote at twenty in "Poem out of Childhood." Here, as throughout her work, the poet's personal memories are knitted together with politics. The word "organize" is significant here, in its activist connotation but even more in its sense of dynamic relational system, a concept that would become crucial to her art and thought.

Her first published poems, in a Vassar undergraduate magazine, invoke New York City scenes and conversations:

"Look," the city child said, "they have built over the river.
It is a lovely curve. But think what that might be:
A circle on that arch would be really something to see!—"

The toll-taker heard, and grinned, and spat. "Lord, what a kid!
Like them all,—wants a good thing to go on and on forever.
Tell him he ought to be glad they made what they did."

Made what they did! . . . I saw the bridge built. One spring
A riveter stood high on the iron skeleton
And the flakes of white fire fell and his hard face shone.

Men strung out cables. They were beautiful,
Cables and men, hard, polished, gleaming,—
The pride that the man-work should now prove fruitful!

The states send automobiles over the Hudson River.
A man stands on the abyss, dropping a penny down,
Breathlessly watching the rush. Stand. The lights of the town

Shine down the Drive, and the grim towers of empire
Are bright, burst, to kindle the evening; the torches shiver,
Flaming high, whirling the city into one strong wind of fire.

—"The New Bridge"

Already, despite awkward phrasings, salient qualities of her work are present: the sense of the great made structures of modernity, creations both of technology and human manual labor; of the makers themselves; and also the minute individual figure against the finished structure. And the child's imagination wanting more. Rukeyser had watched the building of the George Washington Bridge as she was driven back and forth to school along Riverside Drive. She saw it as the consummation of a process, but also as itself altering both the city and the lives of people, of the states beyond the city. She was soon to travel into those states, and farther.

A brief account of the events of her life can only suggest the distances and depths they took her to. Both before and after leaving Vassar she took summer courses at Columbia in psychology and anthropology; she was already involved in the vibrant though far from unanimous circles of the Left in New York, "at the center of a decade," Suzanne Gardinier observes, "whose integration of matters literary and political many of us now can scarcely imagine." She was writing for various periodicals, including *The Daily Worker, The New Republic, The New Masses,* taking part in the debates of the Left, Communist and Socialist, Stalinist and Leninist and Trotskyist—and artistic. "Three Sides of a Coin" in her first book evokes—and interrogates—the mixture of sensual, emotional, and intellectual life in this period.

In 1933 she received ground flight training at an aviation school (a minor, she needed parental permission to train as a pilot, which was denied). In the same year she traveled to Scottsboro, Alabama, to report on a historic case in which nine African American youths were convicted of raping two white women (a conviction later overturned by the Supreme Court and a landmark issue for the Left). There she was jailed for fraternizing with other journalists across racial lines and contracted typhoid fever. At the age of twenty-one she received the Yale Series of Younger Poets Award for her first book, *Theory of Flight*.

The assured voice and materials in this book, its ambition and scope, ran formidably counter to existing traditions of feminine lyricism as represented by Edna St. Vincent Millay, Elinor Wylie, Louise Bogan, or even Lola Ridge and Marya Zaturenska, women poets born in the nineteenth century and writing into the twentieth. In the words of Louise Kertesz, her first critic-in-depth: "No woman poet made the successful fusion of personal and social themes in a modern prosody before Rukeyser." She was also a breakaway from the irony and fatalism of modernists like Eliot and Auden. The young Rukeyser entered, rather, into the company of Whitman, Crane, and, as Reginald Gibbons has noted, Thomas McGrath. She also knew her Bible and Shakespeare and other English poets of the past: "*Think:* poems fixed this landscape: Blake, Donne, Keats" ("Homage to Literature"). In *Theory of Flight* and in the book that followed three years later, *U.S. 1*, she was already in full possession of her poetic powers and her cohering, if variously embodied, worldview. And already, though by nature she rejected the feminine tradition, she was writing as a woman, a fully sexual human being.

In an essay written in 1944 for the *Contemporary Jewish Record* she asserted:

> **To live as poet, woman, American, and Jew—this chalks in my position. If the four come together in one person, each strengthens the other.**
>
> —"Under Forty"

But she also delineated her conflict with the social and political timidity of the Jewish world in which she grew up, her choice of the Jewish ethic she voices in Part VII of "Letter to the Front":

To be a Jew in the twentieth century
Is to be offered a gift. If you refuse,
Wishing to be invisible, you choose
Death of the spirit, the stone insanity.
Accepting, take full life. Full agonies:
Your evening deep in labyrinthine blood
Of those who resist, fail, and resist: and God
Reduced to a hostage among hostages.

The gift is torment. Not alone the still
Torture, isolation; or torture of the flesh.
That may come also. But the accepting wish,
The whole and fertile spirit as guarantee
For every human freedom, suffering to be free,
Daring to live for the impossible.

Published in 1944, the poem reflects on the temptation "to be invisible" offered American Jews even as, in the Warsaw Ghetto, other Jews were resisting, failing, "suffering to be free."

From the first, she was also intensely committed to poetic craft, refusing to let political awareness shoulder it out. Tim Dayton, in his study of "The Book of the Dead," notes that "this concern about developing a command of poetic technique, and that political concerns and consciousness not become a substitute for it, runs through Rukeyser's correspondence of the 1930s and 1940s."

In 1936 she made two very different though interrelated journeys; to Gauley Bridge in West Virginia, site of the (then) worst industrial disaster in American history, and to Barcelona to cover the antifascist "People's Olympics." Turned away from Spain as the Fascists were prevailing, she experienced enough there—including love for an antifascist German athlete who remained to fight and die in Spain—to crystallize her political vision. As she described it years later:

> **I wanted very much for the Communist Party, as I invented it, as I thought of it, to be something that I could be close to, but I was unable to do that. . . . The thing that I wanted most, was the United Front, and I saw that in the first days of the Spanish Civil War, not in Spain proper, but in Catalonia, where socialists, anarchists, Communists, trade unions and gypsies were together in a United Front.**

If the Communist Party U.S.A. was too narrow, too doctrinaire, for her, the greater vistas of a humanist Marxism were not, and as Dayton has shown in a close and critical reading, they deeply inform the central poem of *U.S. 1,* "The Book of the Dead." I would add that they continued to inform her work throughout her life, expressed in her own language.

The next few years found her in San Francisco for the opening of the Golden Gate Bridge, teaching at the California Labor School, writing articles and poetry reviews, working on a biography of the first American physicist, Josiah Willard Gibbs, giving at Vassar and elsewhere the lectures that were to become *The Life of Poetry*. Disinherited by her family, she had a two-month, annulled marriage, bore a son by a different man, and raised him as a single mother. She edited a brief-lived "review of Free Culture" called *Decision,* was witch-hunted as a Communist, was attacked and caricatured by both conservative and "proletarian" literary critics (and praised by poets as unlike as Kenneth Rexroth and May Swenson), went into psychoanalysis with the Jungian analyst Frances Wickes. Besides her life of Gibbs, she wrote biographies of the defeated Republican candidate for president Wendell Willkie, and the English Renaissance scientist Thomas Hariot. She started teaching regularly in 1954 at Sarah Lawrence College, suffered several strokes (see "Resurrection of the Right Side" and "The Wards"), participated in the antiwar actions of the Vietnam era, traveled to Vietnam during the bombing of Hanoi with the poet Denise Levertov, and, as president of the PEN American Center, went to South Korea, where she stood vigil before the prison of a communist poet incarcerated for his writings. She lived to see her poetry rediscovered by a younger generation of politicized women poets and readers, and her first *Collected Poems* in print (New York: McGraw-Hill, 1978). Because she had always pursued a complex and open political vision, she never joined the ranks of disillusioned or right-veering Left intellectuals and artists, even in periods when (as in the late 1940s and 1950s) there was little public resonance for her sense of "the truths of outrage and the truths of possibility."

Rukeyser's *The Life of Poetry* (1949; rep. Williamsburg, Mass.: Paris Press, 1996) is a study of the function of poetry in a time of crisis, an examination of "the outcast art" as a wasted elemental resource in American life. "American poetry," she says,

> **has been part of a culture in conflict.**
>
> **. . . We are a people tending toward democracy at the level of hope; on another level, the economy of the nation, the empire of business within the republic, both include in their basic premise the concept of perpetual warfare. It is the history of the idea of war that is beneath our other histories. . . . But around and under and above it is another reality. . . . This history is the history of possibility.**

Unlike certain essays by poets deploring the marginality of poetry, this is not the complaint of a dissatisfied ego; nor is it the defense of an elite art against the threat of mass or popular culture. It is, rather, a reflection on our social history and literature in terms of "the buried, the lost and the wasted" and the denial of vital relationships in defining who we are as a people. It's an argument against the reification of poetry, whether as iconic or irrelevant; she takes poetry out from the static into the dynamic:

> [A] poem is not its words or its images, any more than a symphony is its notes or a river its drops of water. Poetry depends on the moving relations within itself. It is an art that lives in time, expressing and evoking the moving relation between the individual consciousness and the world. The work that a poem does is transfer of human energy, and I think human energy may be defined as consciousness, the capacity to make change in existing conditions.

She identifies "the fear of poetry" as resistance to such exchanges of energy, such potential—a resistance she traces in American history, in the early colonists' fear of questioning beliefs and divisions brought from the Old World, the fear of "foreignness" and strangeness among offspring of postimmigrant generations, and in "the use of the discoveries of science rather than the methods of science." Science in its methods pursues relationships and flows of energy, though its products, technology, have been worshipped (and commoditized) without understanding of those methods. For Rukeyser a poem is a system of "moving relations" among words, images, sounds: "a web of movement," not of "static mechanics," as she describes the analytic method of the New Critics:

> **The use of language involves symbols so general, so dense emotionally, that the life of the symbols themselves must continually be taken into consideration. In poetry, the relations are not formed like crystals on a lattice of words. . . . Poetry is to be regarded according to a very different set of laws.**

In considering poetic thinking, like scientific method, as one of the essential elements of human power, inseparable from the remaking of society, she goes far beyond any narrow argumentation for or against "political poetry." She does not need to say, nor does she, "all poetry is political."

If Rukeyser had left us only "The Book of the Dead" and *The Life of Poetry,* she would have made a remarkable contribution to American literature. But the range and daring of her work, its generosity of vision, its formal innovations, and its level of energy are unequaled among twentieth-century American poets. Her poems can be panoramic (yet vividly concrete), intimate, epigrammatic, meditative, sensual, mordantly witty, visionary; never are they quiescent or disenchanted. She wrote of sexuality before feminism and gay liberation cleared the space for new sexual honesties, as in poems like her 1938 "Girl at the Play":

Long after you beat back the powerful hand
and leave the scene, prison's still there to break.
Brutalized by escape, you travel out to sit
in empty theatres, your stunned breast, hardened neck
    waiting for warmth to venture back.

Gilded above the stage, staring archaic shapes
hang, like those men you learn submission from
whose majesty sits yellow on the night,
young, indolent girls, long-handed, one's vague mouth
    and cruel nose and jaw and throat.

Waiting's paralysis strikes, king-cobra hooded head's
infected fangs petrify body and face.
emblems fade everyway, dissolving even
the bitter infantile boys who call for sleep's
    winy breasts whose nipples are long grapes.

Seats fill. The curtain's up where strong lights act,
cut theatre to its theme, the quick fit's past.
Here's answer in masses moving, by light elect,
they turn the stage before into the street behind,
    and nothing's so forgotten as your blind
    female paralysis that takes the mind,
    and nothing's so forgotten as your dead
    fever, now that it's past and the swift play's ahead.

Thousands of poems by women, worldwide, have ended in passive posture, in "waiting's paralysis"; this girl escapes submission into the quickened life of art, of a theater moreover where "they turn the stage before into the street behind." And this is not only a women's poem; it embodies—through its own language—the power of art to revive spirit, stimulate consciousness, restore a brutalized humanity.

Rukeyser's work, like that of any really far-reaching poet, was uneven; there are, mostly in her later poems, abstract and rhetorical passages, when she seems to run on automatic pilot. Suzanne Gardinier has observed,

> More than most poets in her country, she wrote in dialogue with the history of her time, specifically with the current of hope for change within it; in the poems she wrote . . . [between 1948 and 1968] when her partner's voice became all but inaudible, there is often the rambling hollowness of a conversation of one.

And yet, in that period she was single-handedly raising her son and writing poems as varied as "Foghorn in Horror" (a shattering depiction of the loss of historical resonance) and "Waterlily Fire":

> Whatever can come to a city can come to this city. . . .
>
> Whatever can come to a woman can come to me. . . .
>
> Whatever can happen to anyone can happen to me.

—a remarkable intuition for a New Yorker, a white and middle-class American citizen, in 1958.

Reading Muriel Rukeyser, writing about her as I have from time to time, I have come to feel more and more the power of her work and presence in American literature—the many kinds of lives and issues she touched, the silences she broke, the voices she made audible, the landscapes she covered. In our own time of crisis, when the idea of perpetual war has dropped whatever masks it ever wore, when poetry is still feared yet no longer marginalized, when a late-1920s schoolgirl's perception of the "grim towers of empire" and "the terrible, murderous differences in the way people lived" accord with what more and more people around the world are experiencing and naming, this poet has readers waiting for her who perhaps, holding this book, will be seeing her name for the first time.

The Baldwin Stamp

A FEW DAYS before the August 2004 Republican convention, I received a letter bearing a new postage stamp—James Baldwin's lived-in, unsmiling face against an impressionistic rendering of a Harlem street. I wondered *why now,* February being designated as Black History Month ("the shortest month in the year," as it's said). Writers and artists, certainly black ones, are not so common on our postage. In fact, the stamp commemorates Baldwin's birthday, August 2: he would have been eighty that year.

I first came upon his work when I was about nineteen, in the old, liberal *Partisan Review*. At that age someone just five years older can seem incalculably so; moreover, this writer possessed both a literary confidence and a life experience far beyond mine. As his essays went on appearing over the next few years, I read them not just eagerly but with the sense of having been thrown—amid all there was for a young poet to read—a lifeline, the sounding of a submerged reality I had been, by upbringing and education, tacitly urged not to investigate. The writings of W. E. B.

Written September 11, 2004, for the *Los Angeles Times Book Review*; revised and expanded in May 2008.

DuBois, Frederick Douglass, Ida B. Wells, and other black American classics were not yet being reissued in paperback reprints and discussed at large, as they would be in the 1960s. Black History Month was not yet officially recognized, nor was the idea of "Black" as opposed to "Negro" or "colored" (or a more brutal term that, I had early been taught, in 1940s segregated Baltimore, was used only by crude and ignorant white people—in my parents' house the term was "They").

I met Baldwin only once, in the early 1980s at a large seminar table at Hampshire College in Massachusetts, where he was then in residence. I remember little of the questions he was asked and courteously responded to. Mostly I looked at the face, listened to the voice, of a writer who had unlocked much for me—certainly penetrating what had seemed unsayable in terms of my, our, racialized existence—but also directing a searchlight on the mental and moral instabilities of my, our, country as a whole, whether in its laws, its folkways, its art, its claims *as* a nation to being "free." He had written of the lives of post–World War II black veterans, whether studying in Paris on the G.I. Bill of Rights or returning to their ghettos carrying the scars of a segregated, racist military (not to mention the experience of war). He had dissected the bad faith underlying Broadway shows and Hollywood movies, their images embedded in the popular mind; the hypocrisy of white liberals and the compromises of black leadership (always identifying and parsing the circumstances that bred them). He had insistently and strategically used the pronoun "we" referring to the American people, of which he knew himself agonizingly a part yet stood off from in his prophetic warnings and his sense of possibility. More than anything, perhaps, he represented for me how a great writer, in full awareness of the limits imposed on his medium by structures that ruled the thinking, education, and consciousness of his potential audience, could employ language to probe and defy those limits.

I did not need to introduce myself to Baldwin nor raise my hand in a question. His work was what I needed.

Worn down over months by the impoverished chatter of political candidates and the repetitive sarcasms of liberal and conservative columnists, I decided to travel, cover to cover, through Baldwin's *The Price of the Ticket: Collected Nonfiction, 1948–1985* (New York: St. Martin's, 1985). Many of these pieces I had read and reread as they were published; others either felt or were new to me. Tracing the writer's movement (and steadfastness) straight through the history of those years sharpened my sense of what's missing from the desperate, hysterical nonconversations in which we've been mired.

Moreover, many passages—on ghettos and their meaning, on how the blinders of "whiteness" have undermined the American sense of reality, on violence and moral balance, on the cognitive dissonance and emotional vacuity spawned by racialism and its secrets, on the interior dread at the core of American triumphalism—seemed uncanny in their prescience.

In America . . . life seems to move faster than anywhere else on the globe and each generation is promised more than it will get; which creates, in each generation, a

> **furious, bewildered rage, the rage of people who cannot find solid ground beneath their feet.**
>
> —"The Harlem Ghetto" (1948)

> **The gulf between our dream and the realities that we live with is something that we do not understand and do not wish to admit. It is almost as though we were asking that others look at what we want and turn their eyes, as we do, away from what we are. I am not, as I hope is clear, speaking of civil liberties, social equality, etc., where indeed a strenuous battle is yet carried on; I am speaking instead of a particular shallowness of mind, an intellectual and spiritual laxness. . . . This rigid refusal to look at ourselves may well destroy us; particularly now since if we cannot understand ourselves we will not be able to understand anything.**
>
> —"Lockridge: 'The American Myth'" (1948)

(So, after the September 2001 attacks, our leaders would inform us that our nation is hated because we are so free, so exceptional, so envied in our way of life.)

Baldwin was a moralist, a role with which many writers today are apparently uncomfortable, since morality has become the hostage of various fundamentalisms, or Hollywood/TV "good guys" and "bad guys," or relegated to the critical trash heap of "post-" discards. But there was no self-righteous or simplistic moral scenario for him.

> **It began to seem that one would have to hold in the mind forever two ideas which seemed to be in opposition.**

> **The first idea was acceptance, the acceptance, totally without rancor, of life as it is, and men as they are: in the light of this idea, it goes without saying that injustice is a commonplace. But this did not mean that one could be complacent, for the second idea was of equal power: that one must never, in one's own life, accept these injustices as commonplace but must fight them with all one's strength. This fight begins, however, in the heart and it now had been laid to my charge to keep my own heart free of hatred and despair.**
>
> —"Notes of a Native Son" (1955)

> **Americans, unhappily, have the most remarkable ability to alchemize all bitter truths into an innocuous but piquant confection and to transform their moral contradictions or public discussion of such contradictions, into a proud decoration such as are given for heroism on the field of battle.**
>
> —"Many Thousands Gone" (1960)

There's a postage stamp for Baldwin now, the year before one for Paul Robeson (depicted as handsome and celebrated singer, not as left-wing activist). We've come a long way from 1960; democracy marches on.

> **The truth is that the country does not know what to do with its black population now that the blacks are no longer a source of wealth, are no longer to be bought and sold and bred, like cattle; and they especially do not know what to do with young black men, who pose**

as devastating a threat to the economy as they do to the morals of young white cheerleaders. It is not at all accidental that the jails and the army and the needle claim so many, but there are still too many prancing about for the public comfort. Americans will, of course, deny, with horror, that they are dreaming of anything like "the final solution"—those Americans, that is, who are likely to be asked: what goes on in the vast, private hinterland of the American heart can only be guessed at, by observing the way the country goes these days.

—"No Name in the Street" (1972)

Thirty-some years later, the proliferation of the prison-industrial complex, the racially slanted drug laws and criminal justice system, and the disproportionate numbers of black men incarcerated and on death row lend weight to Baldwin's grim apprehension.

There is a carefully muffled pain and panic in the nation, which neither candidate, neither party, can coherently address, being, themselves, but vivid symptoms of it.

—"A Review of *Roots*" (1976)

What Baldwin, in 1976, was asking for was more than a half-nervous, half–self-congratulatory "conversation on race." Or gender:

The American *ideal*, then, of sexuality appears to be rooted in the American ideal of masculinity. This ideal

> **has created cowboys and Indians, good guys and bad guys, punks and studs, tough guys and softies, butch and faggot, black and white. It is an ideal so paralytically infantile that it is virtually forbidden—as an unpatriotic act—that the American boy evolve into the complexity of manhood.**
>
> —"Here Be Dragons" (1985)

The complexity of manhood, or of womanhood—of maturity itself—may have become an archaic concept, leaving us to manic posturings of hunks and cheerleaders dressed in the flag. Certainly this has been the impression conveyed by recent political campaigns. But, as Baldwin suggests, our candidates and parties are only symptomatic.

In his lifetime, Baldwin could be viewed as apocalyptic preacher, as instigator to black rebellion, as provoker of "white guilt" (a concept he in fact devastatingly dissected). He was hailed (and attacked) as an early writer of fiction on homosexual experience; criticized harshly for living in Europe while writing on America, for being too much the "aesthete" or too much the engaged writer. He was extraordinarily prolific, writing novels, plays, many volumes of essays and reviews, publishing book-length dialogues, interviews, a volume of poems. At an astonishingly young age he took up, so to speak, Henry James's remark that "it is a difficult fate to be an American," turned on it the lens of black experience—historical, social, personal—and through that lens sought to show himself and his fellow citizens the largest, hardest, most complex truths. He respected James early on as a model and went his own artistic way.

Nurturing and fear in the family, the black Baptist Church, the Harlem streets, his early passion for literature, his sexual desires, the intricacies of what it means to love and what it means to hate (both your own people and the Other)—these were his landscape, and this he grasped as his work as an American artist. More than any American writer I can think of, he had to make his way through the contradictions and temptations of early literary success and tokenization, vilification, and incomprehension that, particularly as a black writer, fell across his path. Determined to remain a real writer and not a mere celebrity or appointed spokesperson, he lived for long periods, and died, outside the United States. He returned to participate in the 1960s civil rights movement somewhat reluctantly, since he saw himself as a writer, not an activist; yet knew he must bear witness to that history as it was being made.

Baldwin held (writing of Langston Hughes) that the artist needs to dwell "within the experience and outside of it at the same time." His own awareness of this difficult positioning (if I am, despite all, an American, what does this mean, for me and for America?) was, I think, a supreme artistic strength, giving him his critical prescience, his narrative powers, his insight into character, his early and vivid recognition of the internal trouble toward which this nation, in its blur of wealth and fantasies, has been heading.

His country has put his face on a first-class postage stamp. Has named a black presidential candidate. But has yet to face its own confusions in his art's unsparing mirror.

Three Classics for New Readers: Karl Marx, Rosa Luxemburg, Che Guevara

If you are curious and open to the life around you, if you are disturbed as to how, by, and against whom wealth and political power is held and used, if you sense there must be good reasons for your unease, if your curiosity and openness drive you toward wanting to act with others, to "do something," you have much in common with the writers of the three essays in *Manifesto.*

They were three relatively young people—Karl Marx was thirty, Rosa Luxemburg twenty-seven, Che Guevara thirty-seven. Born into different generations and historical moments, they shared an energy of hope, an engagement with society, a belief that critical thinking must accompany action, and a passion for the human world and its possibili-

Preface to *Manifesto: Three Classic Essays on How to Change the World—Che Guevara, Rosa Luxemburg, Karl Marx and Friedrich Engels,* intro. Armando Hart (Melbourne/New York/Havana: Ocean Press, 2005), including Marx and Engels, "The Communist Manifesto" (1848); Luxemburg, "Reform or Revolution" (1898–1899); and Guevara, "Socialism and Man in Cuba" (1965). This essay was revised and expanded in 2008.

ties. In their writings and actions all three affirmed that society as presently constructed would have to undergo radical change for such possibilities (stifled or denied under existing conditions) to be realized. They were educated, reflective people who honed their critiques in workers' movements.

Marx lived most of his prodigiously creative life in poverty and exile. Rosa Luxemburg spent years in prison; both she and Che Guevara were assassinated for their intellectual and active leadership in socialist movements. Any one of them might have led the life of a relatively comfortable professional. Each made another choice. Yet reading what they wrote, including the essays in *Manifesto,* one feels not the grimness of a tooth-gritting, dogma-driven ideology (as Marxism is frequently depicted by those it has all too accurately described) but the verve and exuberance that accompany creative indignation. For all three, feeling intensely in the world translated into the vision of an integrated society in which each person could become both individuated and socially responsible, "an association," as a famous phrase from *The Communist Manifesto* expresses it, "in which the free development of each is the condition for the free development of all." Or, as Che told a group of Cuban medical students and health workers in 1960,

> **The revolution is not, as some claim, a standardizer of collective will, of collective initiative. To the contrary, it is a liberator of human will, of human capacity.**

What the revolution does do, however, is to orient that capacity.

Needless to say, none of the three was thinking in isolation or in a historical vacuum. They had the past and its earlier thinkers to learn from and criticize; they observed and took part in social movements; they worked out and argued ideas and strategies, sometimes fiercely, with comrades (Marx especially with Friedrich Engels; Luxemburg with Leo Jogiches, the feminist Clara Zetkin, Karl Kautsky and other German Social Democrats; Che Guevara with Fidel Castro, other Latin Americans, and with leaders of the "nonaligned" nations). They saw themselves not as "public intellectuals" or pundits but as witnesses and contributors to the growing consciousness of a class whose labor produced wealth and leisure for some but who did not share in it—a class more than capable of reason and enlightened action, if often lacking the education that could lead to political power.

That the working people who brought forth the raw and manufactured resources of the world could move toward political and economic emancipation these writers saw as a necessary (if not inevitable) evolution in human history. Revolutions were all around them, mass movements, strikes, international organizing. But it was not just the temper of their times that drew them into activity. (Many professionals, students, writers, especially when young, have been attracted by a moment's flaring promise of social change, only to flinch away and seek shelter as the windchill of opposition begins to freeze the air.) Rather, they observed around them the accelerating relationship between private ownership and massive suffering, capital's devouring appetite for expansion of its markets at whatever human cost—not least its wars. In that awareness they also saw the meaning of their lives.

As a young medical student traveling through Latin America, Che Guevara noted this concretely:

> I went to see an old woman with asthma. . . . The poor thing was in a pitiful state, breathing the acrid smell of concentrated sweat and dirty feet that filled her room, mixed with the dust from a couple of armchairs, the only luxury item in her house. On top of her asthma, she had a heart condition. It is at times like this, when a doctor is conscious of his complete powerlessness, that he longs for change: a change to prevent the injustice of a system in which only a month ago this poor woman was still earning her living as a waitress, wheezing and panting but facing life with dignity.

It was Marx first of all, in *The Communist Manifesto,* who described how capital not only dispossesses and forces the majority of people "to sell themselves piecemeal," but contains, ultimately, its own unmanageable tendencies:

> Modern bourgeois society, with its relations of production, of exchange and of property, a society that has conjured up such gigantic means of production and

> **exchange, is like the sorcerer, who is no longer able to control the powers of the netherworld that he has called up by his spells.**

But he first lays forth an exposition of the history of capitalism, the emergence of bourgeois owning-class power and the effects of that power, a panorama so prescient of twenty-first-century social conditions that it transcends its own moment of writing. As Che was to observe in 1964:

> **Marx . . . suddenly produces a qualitative change in the history of social thought. He interprets history, understands its dynamic, foresees the future. But in addition to foreseeing it (by which he would meet his scientific obligation), he expresses a revolutionary concept: it is not enough to interpret the world, it must be transformed.**

And, in fact, over more than 150 years *The Communist Manifesto* has become the most influential, most translated, reprinted (and demonized) single document of modern history. It's a work of extraordinary literary power fused with historical analysis; a document of its time yet, as we see here, for later generations. A document that can be, has been (even by its author), critiqued and argued with, but that will be carried into any future that is bearable to contemplate.

Marx, Luxemburg, and Guevara were revolutionaries, but they were not romantic. Their often poetic eloquence is grounded in study and critical analysis of human society and political economy from the earliest communistic arrangements of prehistory to the emergence of modern capitalism and imperialist wars. They did not idealize past societies or attempt to create marginal lifestyle communities, but—beginning with Marx—they scrutinized the illusions of past and contemporary reformers, idealists and rebels, aware of how easy it can be for parties and leaders to lose momentum, drift off, and settle down within existing structures of power. (It is this kind of compromise that Luxemburg addresses in "Reform or Revolution.")

So what have we here? What instigated these three essays?

The Communist Manifesto was so named because in 1847 the emerging German Communist League—previously an underground society of exiled radical artisans calling itself the League of the Just—asked Marx and Engels to draft a platform. Both worked on the draft; the document as we know it is held to be Marx's production. Thus, Marx is both setting forth a new theory of history and making a political program *manifest.* He is asking: What in economic history has produced the need for communism as a movement, *and* what, in 1848, does communism actually mean? He describes, with admiration as well as condemnation, the contradictory achievements of industrial capitalism. He notes, sometimes with scorching wit, the "spectral" interpretations of communism floating around in the air and defines its goal as ownership of the means of production by those who create, through their exploited labor and time, the value of goods.

More than fifty years later, in 1899, Rosa Luxemburg vigorously attacks the reformist "opportunism" that would keep old systemic relations of ownership and production in place under the guise of socialist reform. She dissects this opportunism in the ideas of Eduard Bernstein, an elder leader of the German Marxist Social Democratic Party with the additional cachet of being Engels's literary executor. Her confrontation is coming from a young person, a foreigner, and a woman in a party rife with "virulent male chauvinism." Coming from anyone, it would have constituted a probing intellectual autopsy.

> **For Social Democracy there exists an indissoluble tie between social reform and revolution. The struggle for reform is its *means*; the social revolution, its *goal*.**

Using her critique of Bernstein's article as a springboard, she goes on to articulate ideas that acquire renewed suggestiveness today:

> **The fate of the socialist movement is not bound to bourgeois democracy; but the fate of democracy, on the contrary, is bound to the socialist movement. Democracy does not acquire greater chances of life in the measure that the working class renounces the struggle for its emancipation; on the contrary, democracy acquires greater chances of survival as the socialist movement becomes sufficiently strong to struggle against the reactionary consequences of world politics and the bourgeois desertion of democracy. He who would strengthen democracy must also want to strengthen and not weaken the socialist movement; and with the renunciation of the struggle for socialism goes that of both the labor movement and democracy.**

> **Legal reform and revolution are not different methods of historical progress that can be picked out at pleasure from the counter of history, just as one chooses hot or cold sausages. They are different *moments* in the development of class society which condition and complement each other, and at the same time exclude each other reciprocally.**
>
> **In effect, every legal constitution is the *product* of a revolution. In the history of classes, revolution is the act of political creation while legislation is the political expression of the life of a society that has already come into being. Work for legal reforms does not in itself contain its own driving force independent from revolution.**

In 1965, Che Guevara, as participant-theorist of an actual ongoing revolution, writes to an Uruguayan editor-friend a letter obviously intended to *make manifest* the experience of the emerging Cuban society. By then Che, an Argentine, had traveled on his continent, studied Marxism in Guatemala, fought along with Fidel Castro and the July 26 Movement, served in the new Cuban revolutionary government, and was beginning to work with other groups toward the extension of socialism in Latin America, Africa, and Asia. He writes of the labor pains of a transitional revolutionary society. How is it to be born? There is the idea—socialism—and there is also "the human being"—incomplete, potential, coming alive in new conditions where labor becomes shared responsibility, but also initially dwelling, as it were, between two vastly different worlds: **The new society in formation has to compete fiercely with the past.** Commodity relationships are still imprinted on the mind. This phase of revolutionary process is new and unstable; anxiety may seek relief in autocratic rigidity. The leadership in such a transition has need for a vigilant, well-calibrated self-criticism.

Rosa Luxemburg had written: **Revolutions are not "made" and great movements of the people are not produced according to technical recipes that repose in the pockets of the party leaders.** Che envisioned that **society as a whole must be converted into a gigantic school.** Those who hope to educate must be in constant and responsive touch with those who are learning; teachers must also be learners.

In this connection it's necessary to think about art and culture. Marx had described how

> **the bourgeoisie cannot exist without constantly revolutionizing the means of production, and thereby the relations of production, and with them the whole relations of society. . . . [U]ninterrupted disturbance of all social conditions, everlasting uncertainty and agitation distinguish the bourgeois epoch from all earlier ones. All fixed, fast-frozen relations, with their train of ancient and venerable prejudices and opinions, are swept away, all new-formed ones become antiquated before they can ossify. All that is solid melts into air. . . .**

And, in a system of commodity relationships, "the physician, the lawyer, the priest, the poet, the man of science" become "paid wage laborers" who must "sell themselves piecemeal" and are "exposed to all the vicissitudes of exploitation, all the fluctuations of the market." For the artist today this can also mean censorship by the market.

Che elaborates this theme:

> **The superstructure [of capitalism] imposes a kind of art in which the artist must be educated [that is, must be of an educated class]. Rebels are subdued by the machine, and only exceptional talents** [I read this phrase as in ironic quotes] **may create their own work. The rest become shamefaced hirelings or are crushed. . . . Meaningless anguish [and] vulgar amusement thus become safety valves for human anxiety. The idea of using art as a weapon of protest is combated.**

But he also points to the blindness of earlier socialist revolutions-in-process, where "an exaggerated dogmatism" has tried to address the question of culture, demanding "the formally exact representation of nature" in art, followed by "a mechanical representation of the society they [the revolutionary leadership] wanted to show: the ideal society, almost without conflicts or contradictions, that they sought to create."

Che struggles here with the dialectic of art as simultaneous embodiment and shaper of consciousness, rooted in past forms and materials even as it gestures toward a still unachieved reality. What is to be the freedom of the artist in the new society? It can be difficult for those living under the template of capitalist relations to conceive of how a freedom expanded to all, to each and every person, could expand, not restrict, the freedom of the imagination, the artist, and the very possibilities of art. Difficult for those who are already artists—even as, outraged, we are forced to "market ourselves piecemeal" and struggle for what Marx called "disposable time"—to discern the "invisible cage" within which we work. For the cage may also exist within us. Difficult, too, for the navigators of a transitional society to apprehend the peculiar, though not exceptional, labor of the artist.

In the words of the Italian Communist Antonio Gramsci:

> **To fight for a new art would mean to fight to create new individual artists, which is absurd since artists cannot be created artificially. One must speak of a struggle for a new culture, that is, for a new moral life . . . intimately connected to a new intuition of life until it becomes a new way of seeing and feeling reality and, therefore, a world intimately engrained in "possible artists" and "possible works of art."**

The serious revolutionary, like the serious artist, can't afford to lead a sentimental or self-deceiving life. Patience, open eyes, and critical imagination are required of both kinds of creativity. The writers gathered in *Manifesto* all speak emotionally of the human condition, of human realization not as losing oneself within a mass collectivity but as release from the numbed senses, the robotization of advancing capitalist society. Marx writes of "the complete *emancipation* of all the human qualities and senses [from the mere sense of *having*].

. . . The eye has become a *human* eye when its object has become a *human,* social object." Rosa Luxemburg speaks of "social happiness," of the mass strike as "creativity," of "freedom" as "no special privilege," and of "the love of every beautiful day" required to live in a world of struggle. And Che of the revolutionary as "moved by great feelings of love," though this might "seem ridiculous" in the cynical climate of bourgeois politics; of the need for a "new human being," created through responsible participation in a society in which everyone has a stake.

If this is still only a partial, unrealized vision, let us have more of it.

Marxism is grounded in the critical memory of how existing, apparently immutable human relations came to be as they are. The future has an intense need for the past. But this is not a simple relationship. In his idiosyncratic eighteen propositions "On the Concept of History," written as he was fleeing the Nazis in 1940, Walter Benjamin views the ideology of *inevitable* progress toward socialism as a distortion of Marx. Rather, we need the backward vision of disasters and defeats in past struggles for justice to alert us to our contemporary perils. (I have extracted here from Benjamin's much more complex reflections.) In one of a series of articles, "Resources of Hope," Aijaz Ahmad reminds us that "the first resource of hope [is] memory itself." Not to idealize or imitate the past but to comprehend the conditions and forces that have fostered counterrevolution and acknowledge the actual, flawed, too-easily-dismissed victories against exploitation that have been won notwithstanding.

The "finality" that capitalism has claimed in declaring its achievements, the so-called "end of emancipatory narratives" announced by postmodernist theories, cannot be accepted any more than the doctrine of capitalism's inevitable defeat.

In *Manifesto* we hear the voices of people who believed, as antiwar, antiglobalization, indigenous, and rural people's gatherings on every continent have been asserting, that "another world is possible." If for some today this still only means trying to regulate and refurbish the runaway engine of capital, for an ever-growing number of others it means changing the direction of the journey toward a vastly different, still-forming reality. Here are urgent conversations from the past that are even now being continued, among new voices, throughout the world.

Dialogue and Dissonance: *The Letters of Robert Duncan and Denise Levertov*

HERE IS A piece of history, a poetic legacy, that exists partly thanks to a U.S. Postal Service that was at the time the cheapest, fastest communications game in the country. Long-distance telephone calls were expensive and rare, telegrams also (hence the famously curt "Western Union" style). But letters could be exchanged between San Francisco and New York, Maine, or Mexico within two days; unique copies of manuscripts or artwork entrusted to the mails almost without qualm. Had this conversation been talked out on phone lines or had the two poets lived in close proximity, we would not have what's here: an engagement on art, culture, political and domestic matters, and finally a rupture leaving painful adhesions, between two remarkable figures in twentieth-century American poetry.

Robert Duncan and Denise Levertov were committed inheri-

Review of *The Letters of Robert Duncan and Denise Levertov,* ed. Robert J. Bertholf and Albert Gelpi (Stanford, Calif.: Stanford University Press, 2004); first published in *The Los Angeles Times Book Review* (April 23, 2004) under the title "A Poetic Dialogue."

tors of the American modernist poetic movement emblematized by Ezra Pound and William Carlos Williams, and subsequently shouldered by Charles Olson. If Pound was the internationalist of the movement, Williams was the Americanist, locating his themes and poetics determinedly in "the American grain," his sense of American speech, behavior, history, and breath, and his own New Jersey neighborhood. It was to Williams that many young poets of the Duncan/Levertov generation looked as a kind of patriarch, whose blessing they sought, finding each other through magazines like Cid Corman's *Origin*. There Duncan discovered Levertov's early poetry, writing her a poem in response, "Letters for Denise Levertov: An a Muse Ment." Levertov first bristled at what she took as a slur on her work. But soon the two were in intense dialogue.

If Duncan's poem seems an awkward tribute, his use of "Muse" was by no means belittling. In his (still unpublished) *H.D. Book* he was to trace the women who had led him toward poetry: his high-school English teacher in Bakersfield, California, in the 1930s; two Berkeley classmates; then the poetry of "H.D.," Hilda Doolittle (a significant poet beyond the aura of her beauty, her relationships with Pound and D. H. Lawrence, her psychoanalysis with Freud). Possibly he sought another such "muse"—a woman associated with poetry. Levertov, four years younger, born and raised in England, and a relative newcomer to the American poetic conversation, found in him a mentor, an admirer of her work, and for many years an intimate, if rarely seen, friend. But she was not simply his disciple; and she demonstrates, in their long exchange, a growing self-assurance.

Their correspondence, meticulously and generously curated by Robert J. Bertholf and Albert Gelpi, begins in 1953, continuing over a quarter century. During the Vietnam War (which both opposed) the friendship founders over a question resharpened today: the poet's relation to politics, the space for politics in poetry. Or, this becomes the triggering issue, the emotional undercurrent being Levertov's own trajectory, which deeply disturbed Duncan. These were two people of strong opinions on more than poetry. A close, mutually confirming artistic relationship may be like a marriage: until a crisis, underlying tectonic shifts don't get talked out. In our plot-driven world we may assume that the crisis is the "real" story. But I want to focus on how, in these letters, two distinctive artists tried—beyond gender, sexual orientation, politics—to work out, with and against one another, the values and processes of their art. Up to the eventual rift, there was passionate trust in their dialogue, and they bequeathed much to the future, saving almost all of each other's letters.

One striking background element is the uninstitutionalized time in which they start writing: poets emerge and connect, cluster, in odd and chancy ways. No MFA programs, no résumé building, no academic credentials (Levertov was homeschooled, Duncan a 1930s freshman dropout from Berkeley). Though they help each other get readings, share advice on magazines and the few available grants, it's not a career culture in terms of money and professional security to be obtained as poets. The idea is to do one's work, live decently, travel when possible. For Duncan: **The art has to do with what life must be. . . . We are not searching out**

"real poetry," but by our art for a real life (no. 184, p. 272). Part-time teaching, editing, translating, and reviewing pay the bills; urban rents are cheap; a freelance life (especially given a middle-class background) is still livable. Publication by small letterpresses and in marginal experimental magazines is gladly sought. Duncan and his life partner, the artist Jess Collins, eventually buy a house in San Francisco thanks to the monthly income from a trust fund left by Duncan's mother. Levertov, with a less published husband, the novelist and journalist Mitchell Goodman, and their young son, struggles to piece things together. As Duncan writes, with **the light bill, food, installments on refrigerator etc. . . . The dammed money looms large. For all of us**—(no. 82, p. 111). Yet there's also freedom from the enclosures of academia; these poets were each others' workshops. **What I love about you specially is your capaciousness,** Levertov writes Duncan in an early letter **(I love you for reading Wordsworth now, for instance.) Without having anything like your deep understanding and grip of things I do have the same kind of zest for different things, different worlds really . . . your fearless appetite—how timid it makes most people's responses seem!** (no. 26, pp. 39–40). And Duncan: **It's you, Creeley and Olson that always are there for me, . . . whom I imagine when the best is there, when the poem turns one of its wonderful clear things for me, as sharing my joy in the thing made** (no. 52, p. 68).

Among questions to be explored early on was that of judgment, of how to make poetry in a 1950s conformist America where modernist poetics were, like Left politics, on the defensive from the "New" academic criticism. For Duncan and Levertov the freeing of the imagination in poetry was to be realized through form and language, breaking with "verse conventions" (no. 13, p. 19) but by no means through formlessness or mere self-expression. The emergence of the Beats did not overly impress them; though she admired *Howl* (no. 34, p. 49), Levertov found Ginsberg, Corso, and Orlovsky jejune (no. 36, pp. 49–50); both saw Ginsberg, moreover, as hustling celebrity (no. 37, pp. 50–51; no. 41, pp. 55–56). She and Duncan were in accord as to the integration of the life to be lived with the poetics to be pursued. In an early letter Duncan has been reading Darwin's *On the Origin of Species* and suggests: **What if poetry were not some realm of personal accomplishment, open field day race for critics to judge, or animal breeding show— . . . but a record of what we are, like the record of what the earth is is left in the rocks, left in the language? Then what do we know of poetry at all compared to this geology? and how silly we must look criticizing . . . as if geologists were to criticize rather than read their remains** (no. 19, pp. 31–32).

But criticize they did, and many a friend and fellow poet would come under their criticism, whether for bad personal behavior or for writing or abetting bad poetry. Levertov: **Did you like Dorn's poems? I do—in a way—but I've had in the last year (barely) certain revulsions of feeling about his work—it doesn't satisfy me because more and more I need a care for form in a poem. . . . I need poems that have some sculptural quality—not that they should be static but that they should be solid bodies in movement, instead**

of (what so many modern poems are) fluid substances (in movement or at worst stagnant.) . . . The Kelly/Rothenberg/Schwerner/Economou group . . . have more concern with craft, so much more than the Beats . . . and yet their poems do not satisfy me. . . . There is no moral backbone, no sharpness of necessity, in these poems (no. 182, p. 266).

To which Duncan responds: **What I do . . . in response to your letter . . . is to contend. And it obscures perhaps just the fact that I am contending my own agreements often.** He touches on Eliot and Rilke as poets he has wrestled with: **The thing I've found is how my own judgment has shifted. Tho I aim at keeping my consciousness open (my ideal would be an expanding awareness) my appreciations narrow.** But then, the working poet's resolution: **We too if we are to realize some wide and generous risk, to let a poem go out that far to include (you say the whole man)—well some substitute—ersatz, stand-in for we know not otherwise how to do** (no. 183, pp. 270–271).

The texture of the dialogue is thick and various not only in their evaluating of predecessors and contemporaries but in each one's thinking aloud on the page, as it were, about the making of poetry, to a comrade for whom just these matters were of first importance. The letters offer the twenty-first-century reader or working poet a richly provocative discourse: on poetic praxis, on visual art (an important resource for both), on formal strategies, down to the actual placement of lines and syllables. Levertov: **I'm torn between a sense of affirmation of that idea—*not* to revise (not unless it is a complex new see-**

ing) not to polish, to stammer if one stammers, etc.—and my sense of craftsmanship, for the complete (by which I don't mean the closed, the dead.) Maybe the conflict is one of those blissful uncertainties that is fruitful—certainly it's one I've had with me a long time—so I don't want to solve or resolve it—but it interests me to know how far you'd go, or whether your own attitude has changed (no. 86, p. 115)? And Duncan: **I revise (A) when there is an inaccuracy, then I must re-see, as, re in the "Pindar" poem—now that I found the reproduction . . . of the Goya painting, I find Cupid is not wingd; in the poem I saw wings. I've to summon up my attention and go at it. (B) when I see an adjustment,—it's not "polishing" for me but a correction of tone, etc., as in same poem "hear the anvils of human misery clanging" in the Whitman section bothered me, it was at once the measure of the language and the content—Blake! not Whitman (with them *anvils*) and I wanted a long line pushed to the unwieldly with ([Jack] Spicer and I had been talking about returning to Marx to find certain correctives—as, the idea of *work* marxist flicker of *commodities* (C) and even upon what I'd call decorative impulse: I changd**

"~~obey~~ follow to the letter
freakish instructions"

to gain the pleasurable transition of l to l——lr and f to fr.

My "no revisions" was never divorced from a concept of the work. . . . Whatever vitality, you've got just whatever

you have there—but the poet makes a concentration, a focus. I've got to have the roots of words, the way the language works, at my fingertips, learnd in the nerves from whatever studies, in addition to the thing drawn from . . . (no. 88, pp. 118–119).

At first Duncan's are the longer, most discursive letters. Levertov writes more concisely and factually, from a more practically pressured life: she cares for a young son, tends a husband's moods and illnesses, sews name tapes and washes socks, has a brief love affair and decides for her marriage, visits her aging mother in Mexico, looks after her aged father-in-law when he visits, trying to write and read meanwhile. When she finally gets a Guggenheim Fellowship, part of it goes to buy a washer and dryer for the home. Duncan was living with Jess Collins in the homophobically McCarthyite 1950s and 1960s as an openly gay man with a profound desire for domestic civility, for "the hearth," at a time in American life when gay domesticity was seen, far more than today, as an oxymoron. His letters are landscapes or collages of a vividly endowed mind: deeply read, eclectic, contentious, self-referenced often, original, insistent upon a kind of morality of feeling, self-corrective as well. (He condemns not only the Vietnam War but the virulence of Southern racism, has read American history along with Blake and Jakob Böhme.) An exchange in January 1961 gives the timbre of two differently paced lives intensely conversing.

Levertov: **On November 29th you sent me the revised "Risk" and some Emily Dickinson poems. You know, actually those dashes bother me—it seems to give a monoto-**

ny of tone. I can't quite explain it. But if they were actual spaces it would work better for me. I'd like to compare those poems with their versions as usually printed but I don't have an Emily D. . . . There's something cold and perversely smug about E.D. that has always rebuffed my feelings for individual poems of hers. . . . She wrote some great things—saw strangely—makes one shudder with new truths—but ever and again one feels (or I do)—"Jesus, what a bitchy little spinster." (Later she was to revise her view.)

In the same letter, continuing a discussion of poetic imagination: **When this *kind* of imagination—the presence of felt-through absolutely convincing details—is manifested it excites and delights me—shakes and moves me to tears—more than any other single manifestation, I think. I'm sure I don't have as good a sense of the overall drama as you, or Mitch, for instance . . . perhaps it is being a woman. But I have this love of certain kinds of verisimilitude so that even thinking about it in quite a generalized way is almost a sensuous, no, sensual experience, sharp and exquisite.**

. . . It has not been a very productive autumn—I have really *suffered* from a lack of leisure—I sound complaining but it's really been worse than ever before. . . . I became physically over-tired early on—cleaning up before we left Maine, then 15th St—then the tremendous job of the move (packing & unpacking the books and all the things—Mitch was busy painting this place so I did almost all the packing)—and never really regained my energy. . . . (But it's not all physical—I know part of it is boredom with

housekeeping because I can always summon energy to do what I really enjoy!) (Like writing to you—and of course once really engaged on a poem I can stay up all night without any trouble—until the next day at least) (no. 182, pp. 267–269).

Duncan: **The important thing for me in Jerry [Rothenberg]'s work or [Robert] Kelly's thought is that they are searching for their depths; the mistrusted thing is that they have identified "depth" with strangeness.**

. . . It is time to re-iterate what to be radical means, what roots are, what form and image, and service means. That creation is neither conservative nor liberal, but radical. But my mind in recoil goes into a knotted tangle.

. . . I'll not give at all on your sense of Emily Dickinson . . . her work comes through to me without any interfering bother about her personality, and in poems like the one I sent you comes thru as a pure voice. . . .

And I've been fighting about in some paperbag, Denny, of dangers or walls I contend against in the conflicts you present. Dearest Jess, who sees clear (where I try to struggle) says: The major sin is making the arts citadels to be defended or attacked, then our thought becomes military (no. 184, pp. 271–275).

Early in the correspondence, Duncan writes: **We are lined up in the Armageddon of verse conventions against form or poetry. But I don't believe in this battle of the species. . . . As *makaris* we make as we are, O.K.? and how else? It all however poor must smack of our very poorness or however fine of our very fineness** (no. 13, p. 19).

Battles, nonetheless, were to come, grievous as they were, underscoring the quintessential humanness that was there all along.

By 1964, Levertov's letters suggest an increasing sense of her own authority (**I'm not interested in adhering to anybody's rules at this point** [no. 312, p. 445]) as she teaches, edits, begins selecting poetry for W. W. Norton. Letters flow back and forth; the war in Vietnam is intensifying; Duncan writes a furious poem ("Up Rising") that Levertov, increasingly engaged in the antiwar movement, publishes in the *Nation.* In 1966 she writes of a poetic argument: **I stand fast by what has caused me to *feel*. And the range of response in you and me overlaps—& that is a large area—but beyond the area of overlap extends in quite different directions. Years ago that would have shamed and embarrassed me—but now not. You are more the Master, a Master poet in my world, not less, just because I feel that the only emulation of such a master is to be *more oneself*** (no. 376, p. 547). There are other poetic disagreements; then conciliatory and loving letters. Mass opposition to the war is mounting; Mitch Goodman stands trial with others for conspiracy to incite draft resistance; Levertov, at Berkeley, speaks at a demonstration, seen by Duncan on television: he charges her with mistaken and neurotic frenzy, betraying the role of the poet (**not to oppose evil, but to imagine it** [no. 452, p. 669]). She (in one of her longest letters): **I THINK IT IS BULLSHIT WHAT YOU SAY** (no. 453, p. 683). The letters become a kind of embraced wrestling, not just with one another but with passions, beliefs, and vulnerabilities within themselves;

Duncan attacks, Levertov begins withdrawing, silences get longer. By 1975 Levertov, now divorced, has moved into an increasingly public life. In 1978 Duncan attempts reconciliation; she writes first coldly, then regretfully: **your letter came *at least* 2 years too late. . . . There can be a statute of limitations on emotional commitments, though one might like to think in terms of eternal loyalties. . . . I wish it were otherwise, but I can't pretend** (no. 475, p. 717). Ten years and a few brief notes later, Duncan is dead of kidney failure.

But the letters, on both sides, were saved. American poetry—and more than poetry—is the beneficiary. We go on suffering questions they suffered—opposition to official public violence, the ethical dimensions of form, how to love in principled disagreement, the incommensurability of art.

The Voiceprints of Her Language

June Jordan's poetry embraced a half century in which she dwelt as poet, intellectual, and activist—also as teacher, observer, and recorder. To a degree rare among twentieth-century North American poets, she believed in and lived the urgency of the word—along with action—to resist abuses of power and violations of dignity in—and beyond—her country.

To read Jordan today is to read her in a time when reflections of human solidarity, trust, compassion, and respect are in danger of disappearing from our public landscape; when what glares out from public discourse is division—not the great racial and class divides that have afflicted us since colonization, but oppositions marked as "cultural": modernity versus regression, fundamentalist faith versus secular reason. Without denying our cruel separations, Jordan went for human commonality, the opportunities for beholding and *being beheld* by one another. One of her early poems, "Who Look At Me," was originally written for a book of images of black Americans by black and white visual artists.

Foreword to *Directed by Desire: The Collected Poems of June Jordan,* ed. Jan Heller Levi and Sara Miles (Port Townsend, Wash.: Copper Canyon Press, 2005). This version was first published in *Boston Review* (April/May 2005) and has been slightly revised.

Jordan took the world as her field and theme and passion. She studied it, argued with it, went forth to meet it in every way she knew. Along with poems, she wrote children's fiction, speeches, political journalism, musical plays, an opera libretto, and a memoir. But poetry stood at the core of her sensibility. Her teaching began in the 1960s with the founding of a poetry program for black and Puerto Rican youth in Brooklyn called the Voice of the Children; in her late years she created "Poetry for the People," a course in the writing and teaching of poetry for students at the University of California, Berkeley. She saw poetry as integrated with everything else she did—journalism, theater work, activism, friendship. Poetry, for her, was no pavilion in a garden nor simply testimony to her inner life.

She believed, and nourished the belief, that genuine, up-from-the-bottom revolution must include art, laughter, sensual pleasure, and the widest possible human referentiality. She wrote from her experience in a woman's body and a dark skin, though never solely "as" or "for." Sharply critical of nationalism, separatism, chauvinism of all kinds as tendencies toward narrowness and isolation, she was too aware of democracy's failures to embrace false integrations. Her poetic sensibility was kindred to Blake's scrutiny of innocence and experience; to Whitman's vision of sexual and social breadth; to Gwendolyn Brooks's and Romare Bearden's portrayals of ordinary black people's lives; to James Baldwin's expression of the bitter contradictions within the republic.

Keeping vibrations of hope on the pulse through dispiriting times was part of the task she set herself. She wanted her readers, listeners, students to feel their own latent power—of the word, of the deed, of their own beauty and intrinsic value; she wanted each of us to understand how isolation can leave us defenseless and paralyzed. She knew, and wrote about, the power of violence, of hate, but her real theme, which infused her style, was the need, the impulse, for relation. Her writing was, above all, dialogic:

reaching for you
whoever you are
and are you ready? . . .

I am a stranger
learning to worship the strangers
around me

whoever you are
whoever I may become.

—"Things That I Do in the Dark"

She was a most personal of political poets. Her poems could be cajoling and vituperative, making love and war simultaneously, soft-spoken sensual lyrics cohabiting with performance pieces. Yet there's a June Jordan persona throughout, *directed by desire*, moving between longings for a physical person and for a wider human solidarity, vocalizing a range from seductive to hortatory, accusing illegitimate authority along with the recalcitrance of unavailable lovers.

She devised her poems with passion, finesse, and a compressed, individual style. She once defined poems as "voiceprints of language." Hers arc back and forth between manifestos, love lyrics, jazz poetry and sonnets, reportage ("when the witness takes a stand") and murmured lust, "spoken-word" and meditative solos, with mood shifts and image juxtapositions to match.

Snow knuckles melted to pearls
of black water
Face like a landslide of stars
in the dark

Icicles plunging to waken the grave
Tree berries purple and bitten
by birds

Curves of horizon squeeze on the sky
Telephone wires glide
down the moon

Outlines of space later
pieces of land
with names like Beirut
where the game is to tear
up the whole Hemisphere

into pieces of children
and patches of sand

Asleep on a pillow the two
of us whisper we know
about apples and hot bread
and honey

Hunting for safety and eager for peace
we follow the leaders who chew up
the land
with names like Beirut
where the game is to tear
up the whole Hemisphere
into pieces of children
and patches of sand

I'm standing in place
I'm holding your hand
and pieces of children
on patches of sand

—"March Song"

Here she breaks what is actually a dactylic metrical line so that the beat is undermined and countered by the line breaks: a subtle disorienting of form and expectation.

Her flexible, swift mind was tuned to what John Edgar Wideman has called "the continuum of language": intimate lyricism, frontal rhetoric, elegance, fury, meditative solos, dazzling vernacular riffs. These are poems full of specifics—people and places, facts, grocery lists, imaginary scenarios of social change, anecdotes, *talk*—that June Jordan voice, compelling, blandishing, outraged and outrageous, tender and relentless with the trust that her words matter, that someone is listening and ready for them.

She knew many poetries, ancient and modern; her sonnets, for example, are both silken and surprising. But in her preface to the collection *Passion,* she matched herself consciously with the tradition of "New World poetry," non-European, deriving in North America from Whitman, and including "Pablo Neruda, Agostinho Neto, Gabriela Mistral, Langston Hughes, Margaret Walker and Edward Brathwaite."

To read through *Directed by Desire* is to see her, restless in movement, writing always for the voice: sometimes for the intimate interior room, sometimes for declamation. Some of her long performance poems, specific to certain events or written for public occasions, don't survive on the page absent the vibrancy of her live breath and bodily presence. Others do, and will, as "I Must Become a Menace to My Enemies":

. . . And if I
if I ever let love go
because the hatred and the whisperings
become a phantom dictate I o-
bey in lieu of impulse and realities
(the blossoming flamingos of my
wild mimosa trees)
then let love freeze me
out . . .

Some of her brief message poems for friends can seem tenuous and transitory. Others are firmly chiseled epigrams:

There is no chance that we will fall apart.
There is no chance.
There are no parts.

—"Poem Number Two on Bell's Theorem"

In the last years of her life, often in great pain from metastasized cancer, surgery, and chemotherapy, her wit and fury enabled her to go on writing poems of love and polemics, some in delicately caressing language, some grimly or hilariously resistant to diminishment. A late example: the exuberantly scathing rap "Owed to Eminem":

I'm the Slim Lady the real Slim Lady
the real Slim Lady just a little ole lady
uh-huh
uh-huh
I'm Slim Lady the real Slim Lady
all them other age ladies
just tryin to page me
but I'm Slim Lady the real Slim Lady
and I will
stand up . . .

I assume that you fume while the
dollar bills bloom
and you magnify scum while the
critics stay mum
and you anguish and languish runnin
straight to the bank . . .

And she continued to mingle the "conflictual elements" of outraged witness and lyrical beauty:

Because cowards attack
by committee

and others kill with bullets
while some numb by numbers
bleeding the body and the language
of a child . . .

Who would behold the colorings of a cloud
and legislate its shadows
legislate its shine?

Or confront a cataract of rain
and seek to interdict its speed
and suffocate its sound?

Or disappear the trees behind a nomenclature
no one knows by heart?

Or count the syllables that invoke
the mother of my tongue?

Or say the game goes the way of the wind

And the wind blows the way
of the ones who make
and break
the rules? . . .

because
because
because as far as I can tell
less than a thousand children playing
in the garden of a thousand flowers

means the broken neck
of birds

I commit my body and my language . . .

—"Poem of Commitment"

And throughout her ardent, abbrieviated life, she did.

James Scully's Art of Praxis

POETRY IS NEITHER an end in itself nor a means to some external end. It's a human activity enmeshed with human existence—as James Scully names it, a *social practice*. Written where, when, how, by, for, and to whomever, poetry dwells in a web of other social practices historically weighted with enormous imbalances of social power. To say this is not—as Scully's essays vividly demonstrate—to deny the necessity for poetry as an art whose tangible medium is language.

It's a commonplace to say that in a society fraught with official lying, hyperbolic urgings to consume, contrived obsolescence of words (along with things and the people who produce them) poets must "recover" or "subvert" or "reinvent" language. Poetic language may thus get implicitly defined as autonomous terrain apart from the ripped-off or colonized languages of daily life.

It's an even older commonplace to claim "the imagination" as a kind of sacred turf. The appeal to a free-floating imagination permeates discussions of poetry and is traced to many honored sources from Coleridge to André Breton to Wallace Stevens to Barbara Guest. It can assume a degraded public

Foreword to James Scully, *Line Break: Poetry as Social Practice* (Willimantic, Conn.: Curbstone Press, 2005). This version has been slightly expanded.

world to which is opposed the poet's art as an activity-in-itself, distinct from other kinds of activity, work, production, save perhaps as these are treated as metaphor. This is one form of what Scully describes as "social silence":

> What does social silence signify? Withholding what we think from what we say, we treat thoughts as objects, things. . . . In so doing we commodify thought, making it a property. Though what's behind the hoarding, the metaphorical greed, is fear. Social silence is fear.
>
> . . . It might seem that by withholding, or trying to withhold, we refuse commodification. But what is withheld, and from whom? In truth this is not the leaden silence of a Bartleby squatting in the nerve center of commodity exchange, up against the wall, defiant to the end. This silence signifies accommodation, not resistance. Silence is job, career, acceptance. Silence, this silence, is golden.
>
> Consumption occurs through our eating our own thoughtful words: self-censorship.
>
> Language generates a more reverberant, spellbinding, insidious silence than "silence itself" does. Social silence may be projected as speech, writing, data or news. Then words are used reflexively as screens, walls, mirrors facing in on their own ideological garden, which is what they cultivate. They become like Milton's serpent, the silence *within* speech.
>
> —"Scratching Surfaces," in *Line Break*, pp. 68–69

Yet the imagination—the capacity to feel, see what we aren't supposed to feel and see, find expressive forms where we're supposed to shut up—has meant survival and resistance, for poets and numberless others: incarcerated, under military or colonial occupation, in concentration camps, at grinding labor, suffering bleak and traumatic circumstances of many kinds. We may view the imagination as a kind of gated, landscaped neighborhood—or as a river, sometimes clogged and polluted, carrying many kinds of traffic, including pollen and contraband, but in movement: the always-regenerating impulse toward an always-beginning future. Scully addresses the difference in his essay "The Dream of an Apolitical Poetry" through the work of artists such as Gauguin, Woolf, Andrew Marvell, Mahmoud Darwish, and Tadeusz Różewicz.

Most critical writing on poetry in the United States (I can't speak of elsewhere) has reached a pretty low point: degenerated into biographical juicy bits extracted from or read into poems; or "poststructuralist" jargon. Any poet whose work is *both* artistically searching and ideologically dissenting knows how shallow, therefore ultimately dismissive, even favorable critical response can be, isolating poems from their historical and social fields of energy—save perhaps as the poetry can be related to a recognized aesthetic movement. (But aesthetic movements, too, belong to historical and social processes, and need critiquing in that light.)

This is a serious loss for poets (who might benefit from more informed and penetrating criticism); for readers (who might welcome discussion that could bring their reading of poetry into focus with a world they know all too well, help them become the great readers Whitman declared a great poetry would need); and for the trajectory of all whose desire for social justice is inseparable from their need for beauty.

The imagination of an unrealized, humane social order is as passionate and ineluctable as the artist's search for unrealized expression. Scully puts the lie to the idea that one must preclude the other.

I found *Line Break* by chance on the Internet in 2002, searching for Scully's poetry. (He is a poet of the truest kind.) First published in 1988 by a small press in Seattle, it was out of print and already becoming unavailable. Meanwhile, bookstores were stocked with manuals on poetry writing as healing, as personal self-realization, as spiritual self-help—the marketing of some vague panacea known as poetry, a facile solution to an unnamed general malaise.

James Scully's essays, like his poems, refuse to soothe or simplify, to shortchange either poetry or the imperative for social transformation. They are continuously interesting because they take on poetry—and values—from so many angles, are written from a generous frame of reference and in a human voice. In the title essay Scully addresses the work that line breaks actually do:

> **The simplest decisions about line breaks will ramify, affecting not only the structural economy of a poem but its social practice, the way it works *as* a poem.**
>
> **For instance, we know that a line break will influence the way a word or syllable is attacked (in the sense that a musician attacks a note). But the difference between one possible line break and another determines more than whether a particular word is taken in stride or "happened upon." The difference affects not only the work's internal relations, how as an object it**

> **is constructed. . . . When line breaks are shifted, posture and attitude change, along with assumptions about meaning, focus, expectations. The poem "plays" differently.**
>
> —"Line Break," in *Line Break*, pp. 129–130

Elsewhere, questions of meter, free verse, punctuation, and line interact with discussions of liberalism and voice. In "Demagogy in the Musée" Scully unravels the assertions in Auden's celebrated poem "Musée des Beaux Arts" in terms of what is *unmentioned* in the poem, the privileging of distance. Elsewhere, he lays open terms like "ideology," "protest poetry," "dissident poetry," and "poetic freedom." His fiercely demystifying intelligence is grounded in hope and realism for poetry in itself along with other forms of dissident engagement. It propels us into fertile argument with ourselves and others—Scully included.

Curbstone Press has long made possible books like this. It will be good news to many that *Line Break* is back in print. For new readers, in an apparently disconsolate time, it could be a window flung open, letting in necessary air and light.

Permeable Membrane

1

POETIC IMAGINATION OR intuition is never merely unto itself, free-floating, or self-enclosed. It's radical, meaning root-tangled in the grit of human arrangements and relationships: *how we are with each other*.

The medium is language intensified, intensifying our sense of possible reality.

2

Ghostly touch on the shoulder: dust motes of air inhaled, snatch of talk heard boarding a plane, music stored in memory. A smell provokes another sensation, a half-forgotten scene. Dream remnant. "Room sound," as in audio recording.

Working on a draft, I move by touch through what I can't see clearly. My finger on the shoulder of the ghost who first touched mine. As my eyes adjust to dimness, the shape of what I'm doing declares itself. The poem makes its needs felt, becomes both my guide and my critic.

This appeared in a symposium on my work in the *Virginia Quarterly Review* (Spring 2006): 208–210, and is here slightly revised.

Behind and overall there's the interpenetration of subjectivity and social being. Gleaning, not at first consciously selecting. Dissatisfaction, impulse to look at the world anew, scrape at the wounds, refuse popular healings and panaceas, official concoctions. I've learnt how much this work depends on knowing myself—including how astray I can go, have gone, but also trusting how certain poetic choices have taken me beyond any conscious knowing.

I've wanted to write subjective visions of objective conditions. But this sounds like a program. Say rather: Poems become suffused, as the existence, the inner life of the maker must, with what's going on, the breaks in the assumed fabric. The makings of art are rooted in non-art labors—repetitive, toxic, body-breaking, minimum wage or less or none—that everywhere underlie those privileged creations. What you do and don't see. What is seeing you. Eyes in the thicket, eyes in the street.

I need to reach beyond interior decoration, biography. Art is a way of melting out through one's own skin. "What, who is this about?" is not the essential question. A poem is not *about;* it is *out of* and *to*. Passionate language in movement. The deep structure is always musical, and physical—as breath, as pulse.

3

In the culturally stunned, dystopic states of North America a poet needs a different (though no greater) kind of faith and commitment from that of poets under other cruel and t/ruthless political regimes. Faith in poetry itself, more perhaps than has been required in other, older societies. Commitment to a poetics not defined by the market, not complacent courtier verse or prose cut by template. A poetics of longing, of organic necessity.

Mayakovsky: **The presence of a problem in society, the solution of which is conceivable only in poetic terms. A social command.** I read him as saying that for the poet the problem is insoluble by her or him alone, yet he or she feels an urgency to meet it with poetry.

That urgency—emotional as a love affair—is finally the source and meaning of my work. Why go for anything less?

Mayakovsky was writing about making poetry within a socialist revolution: a moment, as it seemed, of widening hopes for human possibilities. The battering of those hopes, both from within and without, was an international tragedy. Here, as "winners" of the Cold War, we're watchers at the bedside of a sick democracy, transfixed and emotionally paralyzed. Public conversation stripped of a common imagination of what's "humanly possible," of human solidarity, of motives other than fear, shopping, and disgust.

In the doorway hovers a waiting dictatorship; let us listen to its language: **We also have to work, though, sort of, the dark side . . . use any means at our disposal, basically, to achieve our objective.**

We want to believe the fever can break, the sick body politic come back to life.

In such a crisis the efficacy of any art is not measurable by its quantifiable mass distribution. If it ever was.

4

There's a permeable membrane between art and society. A continuous dialectical motion. Tides brining the estuary. River flowing into sea. A writer describes the landmass-"stained" current of the Congo River as discernible three hundred miles out on the ocean. Likewise: the matter of art enters the bloodstream of social energy. Call and response. The empathetic imagination can transform, but we can't identify precise loci of transformation, can't track or quantify the moments. Nor say how or when they lead, through innumerable unpredictable passageways toward re-creating survival, undermining illegimate power and its cruelties.

Nor how newly unlocked social energies, movements of people, demand a renewed social dialogue with art: a spontaneous release of language and forms.

René Char: **The poet bursts the bonds of what he touches. He does not teach the end of bonds.**

She cannot teach the end of bonds; but she can refuse to justify, accord with, ignore their existence.

“Candidates for My Love”: Three Gay and Lesbian Poets

To SPEAK HERE as the Kessler Lecturer is a significant honor for me. I’ve pondered a good deal about what I could offer, to an audience of what I take to be intellectual subversives. Along the way I’ll read some poetry by gay and lesbian poets of three generations and talk about desire, community, politics, and love, working through and around those poems.

The threads that grew into the texture of what’s now known as “queer studies” began, of course, not in academia but in spaces opened up by the movements of the 1960s and 1970s, the breaking out from self-denial into self-definition, claiming agency, learning solidarity, arguing a different kind of future.

I’ve been thinking how behind every shelf of publications on gender and sexuality, every course offered in queer or gender studies, lie thousands of ghostly sheaves: leaflets, letters, pamphlets, mimeographed bibliographies, little magazines, posters, movement anthologies, some now preserved in archives, others reduced to landfill. Behind every academic program or lectureship under the rubric of queer studies stand lives that

The David R. Kessler Lecture, given at the Center for Lesbian and Gay Studies, the Graduate Center, City University of New York (2006).

were participant in radical ideas about freedom and justice—movements that moved, in nonlinear ways, into and out of each other. In those movements, queer women and men, unknown at first unless to each other, invisible to their otherwise-comrades, emerged to declare a gay and lesbian politics, because the idea of inclusive justice is—was then—contagious and irresistible. The names Bayard Rustin, Barbara Deming, Lorraine Hansberry, Harry Hay, Martin Duberman, Audre Lorde, Joan Nestle are a few that flash immediately to mind. And, of course, I think of the queer pioneers, Del Martin and Phyllis Lyon, *The Ladder,* Daughters of Bilitis, the Mattachine Society, the early queer underground; the publicly gay, anarchist, antiwar poets Paul Goodman and Robert Duncan. I think, in short, of many lives of defiance and creation.

I came out in early 1970s New York, and the lesbian movement I came out into had been shaped by radical feminism and the Left. Thinking about this talk tonight, I pulled out from its shelf a slender, faded orange book, perfect-bound, basic in design: *Amazon Poetry: An Anthology,* edited by Elly Bulkin and Joan Larkin, published in 1975 by Out & Out Books. In it were gathered thirty-eight poets, some publishing as lesbians for the first time in that collection. I want to read from the editor's foreword:

> **[W]hat *is* a "lesbian poetry anthology"? Some expect only love poetry; others, a collection of poems specifically about our oppression as lesbians. Instead, we have put together a book of poems that show the scope and intensity of lesbian experience. . . . The poems convey**

> **both private joy and pain and a larger context of racial, economic and social inequality.**

A contributor's note suggests something of the political-arts ferment of the period:

> **How to describe the process of waking up from my "painted dream," my childhood in America, and the events that shaped that process: Vietnam, the women's movement, Attica, coming out . . . the strength I found through painting and writing to name myself, working with a community murals group on the Lower East Side and at the Women's School in Brooklyn, to return art to its source, to the very core of people's lives.**

One small anthology in a cross-country proliferation of feminist and lesbian print journalism, magazines, poetry readings, bookstores, film, music and theater groups, artists' collectives, along with women's resource centers, rape crisis hotlines, battered-women's shelters—all this, let's recall, before computer publishing programs, e-mail, cell phones, or the Internet. Technology still meant typewriter, telephone, and copying machine, along with much hands-on physical effort, driven by political, cultural, and physical desire, ardor for change in relations of power.

I don't mean to idealize those years, rather to reaffirm what needs reaffirming now: that radical politics is a great confluent project of the human imagination, of which art and literature are indispensable tributaries. Neither will I try to analyze historically the repeated de-fusions, disruptions, and discountings of liberatory movements—a task for scholars of politics and history. I will say this: we can't just claim we were, in 1980 and beyond, simply outflanked by the material means of the Right, the distorting mirrors of its media. Every historical resistance movement in this country—abolitionist, labor, suffragist, antilynching, civil rights, feminist, socialist—has been up against a powerful and hostile press, not to mention tear gas, fire hoses, truncheons, and vigilante guns.

But the discourse of inclusive justice keeps refusing to be quenched. Its soul goes marching on, stumbling, limping, bumming rides, falling in with the wrong crowd, losing direction, pausing for breath, exhausted, sleeping to dream again—maybe even winning an election here and there.

In the 1980s, AIDS catalyzed a new gay activism, in outrage laced with mourning. The virus took many brave and challenging figures off the scene. It unmasked much liberal homophobia and many contradictions in gay lives and deaths. It brought forth the work and abbreviated the lives of black gay writers and poets like Joseph Beam, Essex Hemphill, Assotto Saint, Melvin Dixon.

And, as Essex Hemphill, poet and critic of gay and straight culture, wrote in 1990:

> **Some of the best minds of my generation would have us believe that AIDS has brought the gay and lesbian community closer and infused it with a more democratic mandate. That is only a partial truth, which further underscores the fact that the gay community**

> still operates from a one-eyed, one gender, one color perception of *community*. . . .
>
> Some of the best minds of my generation believe AIDS has made the gay community a more responsible social construction, but what AIDS really manages to do is clearly point out how significant are the cultural and economic differences between us; differences so extreme that Black gay men suffer a disproportionate numbers of AIDS deaths in communities with very sophisticated gay health care services. . . . We are communities engaged in a fragile coexistence if we are anything at all. . . .

Another poet, Melvin Dixon, addressing OutWrite, the annual gay and lesbian writers' conference, in 1992, had this to say:

> We are facing the loss of our entire generation. Lesbians lost to various cancers, gay men lost to AIDS. What kind of witness will you bear? What truthtelling are you brave enough to utter and endure the consequences of your unpopular message?

So I ask myself, and us—how do we, the beneficiaries of various unpopular messages and struggles, figure in historical losses of momentum, the reversals, the so-called backlash? When and where have we resigned ourselves to, at most, a "fragile coexistence," to political and social atomization, to false choices dictated by a public discourse that mocks the very concept of solidarity?

I know that for myself, in the 1990s, it was not enough to keep going to meetings, demonstrations, to peruse newsletters, talk on the phone with friends. There was a flattening of language, a sense of repetition, or, as I wrote in a long poem:

"That year I began to understand the words *burden of proof*
—how the free market of ideas depended
on certain lives laboring under that burden.
I started feeling in my body
how that burden was bound to our backs
keeping us cramped in old repetitive motions
crouched in the same mineshaft year on year
or like children in school striving to prove
proofs already proven over and over
to get into the next grade
but there is no next grade no movement onward only this

and the talk goes on, the laws, the jokes, the deaths, the way
of life goes on
as if you had proven nothing as if this burden were what you
are."

I needed to remember what had drawn me in the first place toward both activism and political art. The early essays of James Baldwin had given me my first sense of a language—eloquently personal yet public—for the first injustice I had witnessed as a child—segregation, as the whole racial system was named then. Reading his work later, it struck me as one American example of a prose style capable of embracing the bitterest experience, the most prophetic anger, and an implacable knowledge of love. As an artist, writing in that complex "we" he claimed as black and gay American citizen, often self-exiled, Baldwin could be frustrated, bleak, but never resigned. This is from his essay "The Creative Process":

> **We know, in the case of the person, that whoever cannot tell himself the truth about his past is trapped in it, is immobilized in the prison of his undiscovered self. This is also true of nations. We know how a person, in such a paralysis, is unable to assess either his weaknesses or his strengths, and how frequently indeed he mistakes the one for the other. And this, I think, we do. We are the strongest nation in the Western world, but this is not for the reasons that we think. It is because we have an opportunity that no other nation has of moving beyond the Old World concepts of race and class and caste, to create, finally, what we must have had in mind when we began speaking of the New World. But the price of this is a long look backward whence we came and an unflinching assessment of the record.**

Of course I turned to poets, including Whitman, Robert Duncan, Thomas McGrath, Charles Olson, Muriel Rukeyser; but also to the letters and essays of revolutionary socialist writers like Rosa Luxemburg, Antonio Gramsci, Che Guevara, whose undeflected passion for making history put into perspective how frivolous despair can be.

Or Samuel Beckett, writing in 1981:

> **All before. Nothing else ever. Ever tried. Ever failed. No matter. Try again. Fail again. Fail better.**

Did he mean language, politics, or living itself? "No matter. Try again. . . . Fail better" seemed a good idea. And I thought I could translate something of what my country and my friends and I were going through into language—the poems of *Midnight Salvage* and *Dark Fields of the Republic*.

Ideas of freedom evolve, scientific descriptions require amplifying, histories have to be revised. Poetry has a way of resonating beyond its original source moment. Maybe because poetic truths depend not on a structure of ideas but on a medium, not on fixed relationships but on metaphor: lightning flashes of connection. Poetry is a mixed medium: the visual image, the sound, the unexpected relation of words to their accepted usage, or, as Ezra Pound termed them, *phanopoeia, melapoeia, logopoeia*.

I'm going to read a poem from Walt Whitman's *Leaves of Grass*—not the 1855 first edition but the expanded and revised version published in 1891, which includes the section of *Calamus* poems:

Whoever You Are Holding Me Now in Hand

Whoever you are holding me now in hand,
Without one thing all will be useless,
I give you fair warning before you attempt me further,
I am not what you supposed, but far different.

Who is he that would become my follower?
Who would sign himself a candidate for my affections?

The way is suspicious, the result uncertain, perhaps destructive,
You would have to give up all else, I alone would expect to be your sole and exclusive standard,
Your novitiate would even then be long and exhausting,
The whole past theory of your life and all conformity to the lives around you would have to be abandon'd,
Therefore release me now before troubling yourself any further, let go your hand from my shoulders,
Put me down and depart on your way.

Or else by stealth in some wood for trial,
Or back of a rock in the open air,
(For in any roof'd room of a house I emerge not, nor in company,
And in libraries I lie as one dumb, a gawk, or unborn, or dead,)
But just possibly with you on a high hill, first watching lest any person for miles around approach unawares,
Or possibly with you sailing at sea, or on the beach of the sea or some quiet island,

Here to put your lips upon mine I permit you,
With the comrade's long-dwelling kiss or the new husband's kiss,
For I am the new husband and I am the comrade.

Or if you will, thrusting me beneath your clothing,
Where I may feel the throbs of your heart or rest upon your hip,

Carry me when you go forth over land or sea;
For thus merely touching you is enough, is best,
And thus touching you would I silently sleep and be carried
eternally.

But these leaves conning you con at peril,
For these leaves and me you will not understand,
They will elude you at first and still more afterward, I will
certainly elude you,
Even while you should think you had unquestionably caught
me, behold!
Already you see I have escaped from you.

For it is not for what I have put into it that I have written
this book,
Nor is it by reading it you will acquire it,
Nor do those know me best who admire me and vauntingly
praise me,
Nor will the candidates for my love (unless at most a very
few) prove victorious,
Nor will my poems do good only, they will do just as much
evil, perhaps more,
For all is useless without that which you may guess at many
times and not hit, that which I hinted at;
Therefore release me and depart on your way.

I don't want to fix in prose this poem, at once so direct and so evasive, ambivalent and confident. If anything, the poem decoys and dares down that possibility. Certainly its sensuality is heightened by its tone of warning, as it both lures and wards off the "you" it addresses. That "you . . . holding me now in hand" is both singular and—implicitly—plural, and "you" appears to have made the first move ("release me now before troubling yourself any further, let go your hand from my shoulders"). But there's an ambiguity too about the "I/me"—which might at once be the book, the poem, and the sexual body of the poet. ("Look where your hands are. Now," says the voice at the end of Toni Morrison's novel *Jazz*.) The book, the poem, as erotic companion, conspiratorial, dangerous, demanding: ("Your novitiate would even then be long and exhausting, / The whole past theory of your life and all conformity to the lives around you would have to be abandon'd"). More is required of "you" than a quick trick, a fast read. And the "I"—poet or poem or book—is wary, outside the law ("watching lest any person . . . approach unawares").

Here is Whitman himself on the writing of *Leaves of Grass:*

> **"Leaves of Grass" is avowedly the song of Sex and Amativeness, and even Animality—though meanings that do not usually go along with those words are behind all, and will duly emerge; and all are sought to be lifted into a different light and atmosphere. . . . Difficult as it will be, it has become, in my opinion, imperative to achieve a shifted attitude from superior men and women towards the thought and fact of sexuality, as an element in character, personality, the emotions, and a theme in literature. I am not going to argue the question by itself; it does not stand by itself. The vitality of it is altogether in its relations, bearings, significance . . . the lines I allude to, and the spirit in which they are spoken,**

> **permeate all "Leaves of Grass" and the work must stand or fall with them, as the human body and soul must remain as an entirety.**

Don't ask me, the aged and now celebrated Whitman is telling his public, to clean up my book. (On the contrary, he's added the erotic *Calamus* poems.) But what is the element always elusive, the hinted and guessed at, with potential for good and evil? If it's simply how human sexuality is part of the greater texture of the universe or the impossibility of a fixed, single identity—*that* was always affirmed throughout *Leaves of Grass.* I find myself wondering if what eludes "you" isn't also elusive to "I"—if Walt himself isn't speaking internally to Walt, acknowledging what can't yet be imagined, even in poetry. Maybe the intuition of movement through—not beyond—sexual desire to what he calls "amative love" to "the love of comrades," movement toward some future democracy, some evolving complex of relationships?

In his 1970 essay "Changing Perspectives in Reading Whitman," the poet Robert Duncan addressed Whitman's complex effects—"He was a man of contradictions," Duncan says, "and he calls up inner contradictions in the reader." He suggests how superficial is any reading of Whitman as naïvely, optimistically chauvinistic or as displaced by twentieth-century nightmares of exploitation and war.

Duncan writes:

> **Presidents, congresses, armed forces, industrialists, governors, police forces, have rendered the meaning of "America" and "the United States" so fearful—causing fear and filled with fear—in our time that no nationalis-**

> tic inspiration comes innocent of the greed and ruthless extension of power to exploit the peoples and natural resources of the world. . . .
>
> "America," for Whitman, is yet to come. And this theme of what America is, of what democracy is, of what the sexual reality is, of what the Self is, arises from an urgency in the conception of the Universe itself, not a blueprint but an evolution of spirit in terms of variety and a thicket of potentialities.

Now I want to read you an early poem by Duncan himself, from 1946:

"Among My Friends Love Is a Great Sorrow"

Among my friends love is a great sorrow.
It has become a daily burden, a feast,
a gluttony for fools, a heart's famine.
We visit one another asking, telling one another.
We do not burn hotly, we question the fire.
We do not fall forward with our alive
eager faces looking thru into the fire.
We stare back into our own faces.
We have become our own realities.
We seek to exhaust our lovelessness.

Among my friends love is a painful question.
We seek out among the passing faces
a sphinx-face who will ask its riddle.
Among my friends love is an answer to a question

that has not been askt.
Then ask it.

Among my friends love is a payment.
It is an old debt for a borrowing foolishly spent.
And we go on, borrowing and borrowing
from each other.

Among my friends love is a wage
that one might have for an honest living.

In one sense, "Among My Friends" mourns a diminishment from Whitman's consciousness: a narrower, sadder sense of possibilities. Duncan searches beneath the surface of a particular male sexuality in a particular time (post–World War II America, early Cold War, rampant homophobia). He observes, with compassion and severity, what was one kind of gay community, to use our contemporary language. The sorrow pervading this gay maleness is the burden of a sexuality ambivalent with its own desire, doubting the potentialities of mutual love, in the face of external and internalized homophobia: "an honest living" being the needed condition for love.

Duncan had earlier explored what he perceived as gay chauvinism and self-enclosure in his 1944 essay "The Homosexual in Society," published in the left-wing journal *Politics*. It was a courageous, contentious essay, the writing of which he describes as "a personal agony"—"the first discussion of homosexuality which included the frank avowal that the author was himself involved." It was a critique from within, taking the risks that such critiques involve. In making his own sexuality explicit he would be written off by the then-powerful New Criticism poetry establishment; critical of gay self-reference and cliquishness, he would be accused of self-hatred.

But if "Among My Friends" merely documented a certain period and a certain circle, it would not carry, as I think it does, all the way into the twenty-first century, into a dominant culture, not necessarily or primarily gay, where atomization and self-reference are promoted as ways of being—the surface American scene of lifestyles, passionless distractions, trivial choices without deep inner volition, sex without sensuality, irony as emotional distance, money as vocabulary for everything.

Duncan was explicit not only sexually:

> **I picture . . . fulfillment of desire as a human state of mutual volition and aid, a shared life.**
>
> **Not only in sexual love, but in work and in play, we suffer from the . . . competitive ethos . . . the struggle of interests to gain recognition or control, [which discourages] the recognition of the needs and interests which we all know we have in common.**

Duncan had read and reflected on Marx and Dante, Whitman and Jakob Böhme. His poetics and philosophic vision, sophisticated, evolving, sometimes arcane but always radical, were a journey to reclaim the fullness of the senses, the common ground that capitalism as a system of relationships has alienated and declared passé.

In 1973 a lesbian-feminist press collective in Oakland published a long poem by a working-class lesbian, Judy Grahn. In "A Woman Is Talking to Death" Grahn gives chapter and verse to the "death" that is self-denial, accepted disempowerment, passivity, mutual betrayal. ("Death sits on my doorstep / cleaning his revolver.") Stylistically it transits from a long, open narrative line to dialogue to blocks of prose to invocation, from linear anecdote to surreal images. What's notable is the freedom of line and voice, a colloquial diction with surges of intensity. A great public poem, emerging from a new and vital women's movement, expanding the political imaginary of Whitman and Duncan, enlarging the potentialities of gay and lesbian poetry. In sometimes raw urgency, it locates its voice in the class- and race-inflected lives of everyday "common women."

Here are just a few excerpts.

A Woman Is Talking to Death

Testimony in trials that never got heard

my lovers teeth are white geese flying above me
my lovers muscles are rope ladders under my hands

we were driving home slow
my lover and I, across the long Bay Bridge,
one February midnight, when midway
over in the far left lane, I saw a strange scene:

one small young man standing by the rail,
and in the lane itself, parked straight across
as if it could stop anything, a large young
man upon a stalled motorcycle, perfectly
relaxed as if he'd stopped at a hamburger stand;
he was wearing a peacoat and levis, and
he had his head back, roaring, you
could almost hear the laugh, it
was so real.

"Look at that fool," I said, "in the
middle of the bridge like that," a very
womanly remark.

Then we heard the meaning of the noise
of metal on a concrete bridge at 50
miles an hour, and the far left lane
filled up with a big car that had a
motorcycle jammed on its front bumper, like
the whole thing would explode; the friction
sparks shot up bright orange for many feet
into the air, and the racket still sets
my teeth on edge.

When the car stopped we stopped parallel
and Wendy headed for the callbox while I
ducked across those 6 lanes like a mouse
in the bowling alley. "Are you hurt?" I said,
the middle-aged driver had the greyest black face,
"I couldn't stop, I couldn't stop, what happened?"

Then I remembered. "Somebody," I said, "was *on*
the motorcycle." I ran back,
one block? two blocks? the space for walking
on the bridge is maybe 18 inches, whoever
engineered this arrogance. in the dark
stiff wind it seemed I would
be pushed over the rail, would fall down
screaming onto the hard surface of
the bay, but I did not, I found the tall young man
who thought he owned the bridge, now lying on
his stomach, head cradled in his broken arm.

He had glasses on, but somewhere he had lost
most of his levis, where were they?
and his shoes. Two short cuts on his buttocks,
that was the only mark except his thin white
seminal tubes were all strung out behind; no
child left in him; and he looked asleep.

I plucked wildly at his wrist, then put it
down; there were two long haired women
holding back the traffic just behind me
with their bare hands, the machines came
down like mad bulls, I was scared, much
more than usual, I felt easily squished
like the earthworms crawling on a busy
sidewalk after the rain; *I wanted to*
leave. And met the driver, walking back.

"The guy is dead." I gripped his hand,
the wind was going to blow us off the bridge.

"Oh my God," he said, "haven't I had enough
trouble in my life?" He raised his head,
and for a second was enraged and yelling,
at the top of the bridge—"I was just driving
home!" His head fell down. "My God, and
now I've killed somebody."

. . . .

I had a woman waiting for me,
in her car and in the middle of the bridge,
I'm frightened, I said,
I'm afraid, he said, stay with me,
please don't go, stay with me, be
my witness—"No," I said, "I'll be your
witness—later," and I took his name
and number, "but I can't stay with you,
I'm too frightened of the bridge, besides
I have a woman waiting
and no license—
and no tail lights—"
so I left—
As I have left so many of my lovers.

we drove home
shaking, Wendy's face greyer
than any white person's I have ever seen.

. . . .

that same week I looked into the mirror
and nobody was there to testify;

how clear, an unemployed queer woman
makes no witness at all,
nobody at all was there for
those two questions: what does
she do, and who is she married to?

I am the woman who stopped on the bridge
and this is the man who was there
our lovers teeth are white geese flying
above us, but we ourselves are
easily squished.

. . . .

death sits on my doorstep
cleaning his revolver
death cripples my feet and sends me out
to wait for the bus alone,
then comes by driving a taxi.

. . . .

this woman is a lesbian, be careful.

When I was arrested and being thrown out
of the military, the order went out: dont anybody
speak to this woman, and for those three
long months, almost nobody did;   the dayroom, when
I entered it, fell silent til I had gone; they
were afraid, they knew the wind would blow
them over the rail, the cops would come,
the water would run into their lungs.

Everything I touched
was spoiled. They were my lovers, those
women, but nobody had taught us to swim.
I drowned, I took 3 or 4 others down
when I signed the confession of what we
had done   together.

No one will ever speak to me again.

. . . .

Have you ever committed any indecent acts with women?

Yes, many. I am guilty of allowing suicidal women to die before my eyes or in my ears or under my hands because I thought I could do nothing. I am guilty of leaving a prostitute who held a knife to my friend's throat to keep us from leaving, because we would not sleep with her, we thought she was old and fat and ugly; I am guilty of not loving her who needed me; I regret all the women I have not slept with or comforted, who pulled themselves away from me for lack of something I had not the courage to fight for, for us, our life, our planet, our city, our meat and potatoes, our love. These are indecent acts, lacking courage, lacking a certain fire behind the eyes, which is the symbol, the raised fist, the sharing of resources, the resistance that tells death he will starve for the lack of us, our extra. Yes I have committed acts of indecency with women and most of them were acts of omission. I regret them bitterly.

. . . .

my lovers teeth are white geese flying above me
my lovers muscles are rope ladders under my hands
we are the river of life and the fat of the land
death, do you tell me I cannot touch this woman?
if we use each other up
on each other
that's a little bit less for you
a little bit less for you, ho
death, ho ho death.

. . . .

to my lovers I bequeath
the rest of my life

I want nothing left of me for you, ho death
except some fertilizer
for the next batch of us
who do not hold hands with you
who do not embrace you
who try not to work for you
or sacrifice themselves or trust
or believe in you, ho ignorant
death, how do you know
we happened to you?

wherever our meat hangs on our own bones
for our own use
your pot is so empty
death, ho death
you shall be poor

Grahn herself wrote of the poem:

> **The particular challenges . . . for me were . . . the criss-cross oppressions which . . . continually divide us—and how to define a lesbian life within the context of other people in the world. I did not realize at the time that I was also taking up the subject of heroes in a modern life which for many people is more like a war than not, or that I would begin a redefinition for myself of the subject of love.**

There is no "progress"—political or otherwise—in poetry—only riffs, echoes, of many poems and poets speaking into the future and back toward the past. Breaking with one tradition to discover another. Returning to an abandoned tradition, like an abandoned house, to find it inhabited by new guests. The poems I chose to read tonight are in their very different ways parts of that continuum.

I will end by thanking you for the opportunity to take this backward look at some of the writings and movements that got us here and to think again, for myself, and in your presence, about sexuality, poetry, community, politics, and what love has to do with all these.

Poetry and the Forgotten Future

1

POETS, READERS OF poetry, strangers, and friends, I'm honored and glad to be here among you.

There's an invisible presence in this room whom I want to invoke: the great Scottish Marxist bard Hugh MacDiarmid. I'll begin by reading from his exuberant, discursive manifesto called, bluntly, "The Kind of Poetry I Want." I'll offer a few extracts and hope you'll read the whole poem for yourselves:

A poetry the quality of which
Is a stand made against intellectual apathy,
Its material founded, like Gray's, on difficult knowledge
And its metres those of a poet
Who has studied Pindar and Welsh poetry,
But, more than that, its words coming from a mind
Which has experienced the sifted layers on layers
Of human lives—aware of the innumerable dead
And the innumerable to-be-born . . .

Plenary Lecture, Conference on Poetry and Politics, University of Stirling, Scotland, July 13, 2006. First published in 2007 as *Poetry and Commitment,* a chapbook, by W. W. Norton & Company.

A speech, a poetry, to bring to bear upon life
The concentrated strength of all our being . . .

Is not this what we require?— . . .
A fineness and profundity of organization
Which is the condition of a variety enough
To express all the world's . . .

In photographic language, "wide-angle" poems . . .
A poetry like an operating theatre
Sparkling with a swift, deft energy,
Energy quiet and contained and fearfully alert,
In which the poet exists only as a nurse during an operation
. . .

A poetry in which the images
Work up on each other's shoulders like Zouave acrobats,
Or strange and fascinating as the Javanese dancer,
Retna Mohini, or profound and complicated
Like all the work of Ram Gopal and his company . . .

Poetry of such an integration as cannot be effected
Until a new and conscious organization of society
Generates a new view
Of the world as a whole . . .

—A learned poetry wholly free
of the brutal love of ignorance;
And the poetry of a poet with no use
For any of the simpler forms of personal success.

A manifesto of desire for "a new and conscious organization of society" and a poetic view to match it. A manifesto that acknowledges the scope, tensions, and contradictions of the poet's undertaking. Let's bear in mind the phrases "difficult knowledge," "the concentrated strength of all our being," the poem as "wide-angled," but also the image of the poet as nurse in the operating theater: "fearfully alert."

2

What I'd like to do here is touch on some aspects of poetry as it's created and received in an even more violently politicized and brutally divided world than the one MacDiarmid knew. This won't be a shapely lecture; rather, I'll be scanning the terrain of poetry and commitment with many jump-cuts, hoping some of this may rub off in other sessions and conversations.

To begin: what do I mean by commitment?

I'll flash back to 1821: Shelley's claim, in "The Defence of Poetry," that "poets are the unacknowledged legislators of the world." Piously overquoted, mostly out of context, it's taken to suggest that simply by virtue of composing verse, poets exert some exemplary moral power—in a vague, unthreatening way. In fact, in his earlier political essay "A Philosophic View of Reform," Shelley had written that "Poets *and philosophers* [italics mine] are the unacknowledged" etc. The philosophers he was talking about were revolutionary-minded: Thomas Paine, William Godwin, Voltaire, Mary Wollstonecraft.

And Shelley was, no mistake, out to change the legislation of his time. For him there was no contradiction among poetry, political philosophy, and active confrontation with illegitimate authority. This was perfectly apparent to the reviewer in the *High Tory Quarterly* who mocked him as follows:

> Mr. Shelley would abrogate our laws. . . . He would abolish the rights of property. . . . He would pull down our churches, level our Establishment, and burn our bibles. . . .

His poem "Queen Mab," denounced and suppressed when first printed, was later pirated in a kind of free-speech movement and sold in cheap editions on street stalls in the industrial neighborhoods of Manchester, Birmingham, and London. There, it found plenty of enthusiastic readers among a literate working and middle class of trade unionists and Chartists. In it, Queen Mab surveys the world's disorders and declares:

> This is no unconnected misery,
> Nor stands uncaused and irretrievable.
> Man's evil nature, that apology
> Which kings who rule and cowards who crouch, set up
> For their unnumbered crimes, sheds not the blood
> Which desolates the discord-wasted land.
>
> . . . .

NATURE!—No!
Kings, priests and statesmen blast the human flower. . . .

Shelley, in fact, saw powerful institutions, not original sin or "human nature," as the source of human misery. For him, art bore an integral relationship to the "struggle between Revolution and Oppression." His West Wind was the "trumpet of a prophecy," driving "dead thoughts . . . like withered leaves, to quicken a new birth."

He did *not* say, "Poets are the unacknowledged interior decorators of the world."

3

Pursuing this theme of the committed poet and the action of poetry in the world: two interviews, both from 1970.

A high official of the Greek military junta asks the poet Yannis Ritsos, then under house arrest: "You are a poet. Why do you get mixed up in politics?"

Ritsos answers, "A poet is the first citizen of his country and for this very reason it is the duty of the poet to be concerned about the politics of his country."

A Communist, he had been interned in fascist prison camps from 1947 to 1953; one of his books was publicly burned. For most of his countrymen he was indeed a "first citizen," a voice for a nation battered by invasion, occupation, and civil war—in poems of densely figurative beauty. As such, he was also a world citizen. His long poem "Romiosini," from its own place and era, speaks to the wars and military occupations of the twenty-first century (I extract from Kimon Friar's translation):

This landscape is as harsh as silence,
it hugs to its breast the scorching stones,
clasps in the light its orphaned olive trees and vineyards,
clenches its teeth. There is no water. Light only.
Roads vanish in light and the shadow of the sheepfold is made of iron.

Trees, rivers, and voices have turned to stone in the sun's quicklime.
Roots trip on marble. Dust-laden lentisk shrubs.
Mules and rocks. All panting. There is no water.
All are parched. For years now. All chew a morsel of sky to choke down
their bitterness. . . .

In the field the last swallow had lingered late,
balancing in the air like a black ribbon on the sleeve of autumn.
Nothing else remained. Only the burned houses smouldering still.

The others left us some time ago to lie under the stones,
with their torn shirts and their vows scratched on the fallen door.
No one wept. We had no time. Only the silence grew deeper still. . . .

It will be hard for us to forget their hands,
it will be hard for hands calloused on a trigger to question a daisy. . . .

Every night in the fields the moon turns the magnificent dead over on their backs,
searching their faces with savage, frozen fingers to find her son
by the cut of his chin and his stony eyebrows,
searching their pockets. She will always find something. There is
always something to find.

A locket with a splinter of the Cross. A stubbed-out cigarette.
A key, a letter, a watch stopped at seven.
We wind up the watch again. The hours plod on . . .

This was Greece speaking; today it could be Gaza or Iraq, Afghanistan or Lebanon.

Second interview. The South African poet Dennis Brutus, when asked about poetry and political activity: "I believe that the poet—as a poet—has no obligation to be committed, but the man—as a man—has an obligation to be committed. What I'm saying is that I think everybody ought to be committed and the poet is just one of the many 'everybodies.'"

Dennis Brutus wrote, acted on, was imprisoned then exiled for his opposition to the South African apartheid regime. And he continues to act and write in the international sphere in movements for global economic justice. I'll read one epigrammatically terse poem—not typical of his work but expressing a certain point:

An old black woman,
suffering,
tells me I have given her
"new images"

—a father bereaved
by radical heroism
finds consolation
in my verse.

then I know
these are those I write for
and my verse works.

My verse works. In two senses: as participant in political struggle, and at the personal, visceral level where it's received and its witness acknowledged. These are two responses to the question of poetry and commitment, which I take as complementary, not in opposition.

What's at stake here is the recognition of poetry as what James Scully calls "social practice." He distinguishes between "protest poetry" and "dissident poetry": Protest poetry is "conceptually shallow," "reactive," predictable in its means, too often a hand-wringing from the sidelines.

Dissident poetry, however [he writes] **does not respect**

boundaries between private and public, self and other. In breaking boundaries, it breaks silences, speaking for, or at best, with, the silenced; opening poetry up, putting it into the middle of life. . . . It is a poetry that talks back, that would act as part of the world, not simply as a mirror of it.

4

I'm both a poet and one of the "everybodies" of my country. I live, in poetry and daily experience, with manipulated fear, ignorance, cultural confusion, and social antagonism huddling together on the fault line of an empire. In my lifetime I've seen the breakdown of rights and citizenship where ordinary "everybodies," poets or not, have left politics to a political class bent on shoveling the elemental resources, the public commons of the entire world, into private control. Where democracy has been left to the raiding of "acknowledged" legislators, the highest bidders. In short, to a criminal element.

Ordinary, comfortable Americans have looked aside when our fraternally-twinned parties—Democrat and Republican—have backed dictatorships against popular movements abroad; as their covert agencies, through torture and assassination, through supplied weapons and military training, have propped up repressive parties and regimes in the name of anticommunism and our "national interests." Why did we think fascistic methods, the subversion of civil and human rights, would be contained somewhere else? Because as a nation, we've clung to a self-righteous false innocence, eyes shut to our own scenario, our body politic's internal bleeding.

But internal bleeding is no sudden symptom. That uncannily prescient African American writer James Baldwin asked his country, a quarter century ago: "If you don't know my father, how can you know the people in the streets of Tehran?"

This year, a report from the Bureau of Justice Statistics finds that 1 out of every 136 residents of the United States is behind bars: many in jails, unconvicted. That the percentage of black men in prison or jail is almost 12 to 1 over white male prisoners. That the states with the highest rates of incarceration and execution are those with the poorest populations.

We often hear that—by contrast with, say, Nigeria or Egypt, China or the former Soviet Union—the West doesn't imprison dissident writers. But when a nation's criminal justice system imprisons so many—often on tawdry evidence and botched due process—to be tortured in maximum security units or on death row, overwhelmingly because of color and class, it is in effect—and intention—silencing potential and actual writers, intellectuals, artists, journalists: a whole intelligentsia. The internationally known case of Mumia Abu-Jamal is emblematic but hardly unique. The methods of Abu Ghraib and Guantánamo have long been practiced in the prisons and policing of the United States.

What has all this to do with poetry? Would we have come here, from so many directions, to such a conference if "all this" had nothing to do with poetry? (We can also imagine others who might be here if not for the collision of politics with literature.) In the words of Brecht's Galileo, addressed to scientists in a newly commercial age, but equally challenging for artists: What are we working *for?*

But—let's never discount it—within every official, statistical, designated nation, there breathes another nation: of unappointed, unappeased, unacknowledged clusters of people who daily, with fierce imagination and tenacity, confront cruelties, exclusions, and indignities, signaling through those barriers—which are often literal cages—in poetry, music, street theater, murals, videos, Web sites—and through many forms of direct activism.

And this keeps happening: I began making notes for this talk last March, on a day of cold wind, flattened white light overhanging the coast where I live. Raining for almost a month. A numbing sense of dead-end, endless winter, endless war.

In the last week of March, a punitive and cynical anti-immigrant bill is introduced in Congress and passed by the House of Representatives. As most of you know, essential sectors of the Western economies depend on the low-wage labor and social vulnerability of economic refugees—especially, in the United States, from south of the border. That bill would make it a felony not just to employ, but to give medical aid, even food or water, to an "illegal" immigrant. Between the United States and Mexico, a walled, armed border would turn back those economic refugees. The hypocrisy and flagrant racism of that bill arouses a vast population. Community leaders put out the word, call the Spanish-language radio stations to announce protest gatherings. Suddenly—though such events are never really sudden—a massive series of oppositional marches pours into the streets of Los Angeles,

Chicago, New York, Detroit, Atlanta, Denver, Houston, and other large and smaller cities and towns—the largest demonstrations in the history of many of those cities. Not only people from Mexico and Central America, but immigrant groups from Asia, Africa, the Caribbean, the Philippines, from Arab-American communities: families, students, activists, unions, clergy, many at risk of firing or deportation, opposing that bill. Millions of people. A working-class movement different from earlier movements. A new articulation of dignity and solidarity. And a new politicized generation growing in part out of those marches—in, for example, a coalition of young Latinos and African Americans.

Of course, there's the much larger political resistance heating up—let me simply mention Chiapas, Seattle, Buenos Aires, Genoa, Porto Alegre, Caracas, Mumbai, the streets of Paris and other European cities—not to mention worldwide women's and indigenous people's movements, which have never gone away—and the gay and lesbian liberation movements allied with, and often emerging from, these.

5

I hope never to idealize poetry—it has suffered enough from that. Poetry is not a healing lotion, an emotional massage, a kind of linguistic aromatherapy. Neither is it a blueprint, nor an instruction manual, nor a billboard. There is no universal Poetry anyway, only poetries and poetics, and the streaming, intertwining histories to which they belong. There is room, indeed necessity, for both Neruda and César Vallejo, for Pier

Paolo Pasolini and Alfonsina Storni, for Audre Lorde and Aimé Césaire, for both Ezra Pound and Nelly Sachs. Poetries are no more pure and simple than human histories are pure and simple. Poetry, like silk or coffee or oil or human flesh, has had its trade routes. And there are colonized poetics and resilient poetics, transmissions across frontiers not easily traced.

Walt Whitman never separated his poetry from his vision of American democracy—a vision severely tested in a Civil War fought over the economics of slavery. Late in life he called "poetic lore . . . a conversation overheard in the dusk, from speakers far or hid, of which we get only a few broken murmurs"—the obscurity, we might think now, of democracy itself.

But also of those "dark times" in and about which Bertolt Brecht assured us there would be songs.

Poetry has been charged with "aestheticizing," thus being complicit in, the violent realities of power, of practices like collective punishment, torture, rape, and genocide. This accusation was famously invoked in Adorno's "after the Holocaust lyric poetry is impossible"—which Adorno later retracted and which a succession of Jewish poets have in their practice rejected. I'm thinking now not only of post–World War II poets like Paul Celan, Edmond Jabès, Nelly Sachs, Kadia Molodowsky, Muriel Rukeyser, Irena Klepfisz. I'm also thinking of contemporary poems in a recent collection from Israel that I've been reading in translation: *With an Iron Pen: Twenty Years of Hebrew Protest Poetry,* ignited by the atrocious policies and practices of Israel's occupation of Palestine. There, poems of dissonant, harsh beauty, some thrusting images of the Occupation into the very interior of Israeli domestic life:

> **. . . I open the refrigerator door**
> **and see a weeping roll,**
> **see a piece of bleeding cheese,**
> **a radish forced to sprout**
> **by shocks from wires**
> **and blows from fists.**
> **The meat on its plate**
> **tells of placentas**
> **cast aside by roadblocks. . . .**
>
> —Aharon Shabtai, "The Fence," trans. Peter Cole

—or suggesting how the poem itself endures its own knowledge:

> **The poem isn't served meat and fruit**
> **on a silver platter at night,**
> **and by day its mouth does not long**
> **for a golden spoon or communion wafers.**
> **Lost, it wanders the roads of Beit Jala,**
> **sways like a drunk through the streets of Bethlehem,**
> **seeking you along the way in vain,**
> **searching for your shadow's shadow in the shrubs.**
>
> **Close to the breast, the soul sits**
> **curled up like a boy in a sleeping bag**
> **dry as a flower bulb buried in the middle of the throat.**

Then the poem feels it can't go on any longer
wandering towards the refugee camp,
toward the fugitives' cradle
in the Promised Land's heavy summer
on the path to disaster

—Rami Saari, "Searching the Land," trans. Lisa Katz

Do poems like these "work"? How do we calculate such a thing on a day when Israel is battering its way into Gaza, bombing Lebanon? Like the activist, the poet (who may be both) has to reckon with disaster, desperation, and exhaustion—these, too, are the materials.

And in such a time—when water is poisoned, when sewage flows into houses, when air becomes unbreathable from the dust of blasted schools and hospitals—poetry must gasp for breath.

But if poetry had gone mute after every genocide in history, there would be no poetry left in the world, and this conference might have a different theme: "The Death of the Poem" perhaps?

If to "aestheticize" is to glide across brutality and cruelty, treat them merely as dramatic occasions for the artist rather than structures of power to be revealed and dismantled—much hangs on the words "merely" and "rather than." Opportunism isn't the same as committed attention. But we can also define the "aesthetic" not as a privileged and sequestered rendering of human suffering, but as news of an awareness, a resistance, that totalizing systems want to quell: art reaching into us for what's still passionate, still unintimidated, still unquenched.

Poetry has been written off on other counts: (1) it's not a mass-market "product": it doesn't get sold on airport newsstands or in supermarket aisles; (2) the actual consumption figures for poetry can't be quantified at the checkout counter; (3) it's too "difficult" for the average mind; (4) it's too elite, but the wealthy don't bid for it at Sotheby's. It is, in short, redundant. This might be called the free-market critique of poetry.

There's actually an odd correlation between these ideas: poetry is either inadequate, even immoral, in the face of human suffering, or it's unprofitable, hence useless. Either way, poets are advised to hang our heads or fold our tents. Yet in fact, throughout the world, transfusions of poetic language can and do quite literally keep bodies and souls together—and more.

Two items from recent news. One is a headline from the *San Francisco Chronicle* of July 17, 2005:

Writing Poetry Was the Balm That Kept Guantanamo Prisoners from Going Mad

The story follows of a Pakistani Muslim, Abdul Rahim Dost, arrested in Afghanistan and held without charges in the American detention camp at Guantánamo. There he wrote thousands of lines in Pashto, translated Arabic poetry into Pashto, at first scratching lines with his fingernail into Styrofoam cups. His brother and fellow inmate is quoted as saying that "poetry was our support and psychological uplift. . . . Many people have lost their minds there. I know 40 or 50 prisoners who are mad."

These men, detained as terrorists (released after three years), turned to poetry in the depths of Guantánamo to keep themselves sane, hold onto a sense of self and culture. So, too, the Chinese immigrants to California in the early twentieth century, detained in barracks on an island in San Francisco Bay, traced their ideograms of anger and loneliness on the walls of that prison.

But poetry sometimes also finds those who weren't looking for it.

From the Israeli newspaper *Haaretz* of November 7, 2004, comes an article by David Zonsheine, a former commander in the Israel Defense Force who became organizer and leader of the anti-Occupation movement within the IDF, the Courage to Refuse. Zonsheine comes by chance upon some lines from a poem of Yitzhak Laor and finds that

> **reading these lines a moment after a violent month of reserve duty, which was full of a sense of the righteousness of the way, was no easy thing. I remember that for one alarming moment I felt that I was looking at something I was forbidden to see. What this thing was I did not know, but on that same Friday afternoon I went out to look for every book by Yitzhak Laor that I could find in the shops.**

Zonsheine continues,

> **The sense of mission with which I enlisted in the IDF was based . . . on . . . the painfully simple message that we shall not allow the Holocaust of the Jews to**

repeat itself no matter what the costs, and when the moral price became more severe, the sense of mission only increased . . . I am a freedom fighter . . . not an occupier, not cruel, certainly not immoral . . .

Something in Laor's texts spoke to me about the place inside me that had been closed and denied until then . . .

Here I am, 28 years old, returning home from another month of reserve duty in Gaza and suddenly asking myself questions that are beginning to penetrate even the armor of the righteousness . . . in which they had dressed me years ago. And Laor's strong words return to echo in my ears: "With such obedience? With such obedience? With such obedience?"

Ever since I refused to serve in the territories and the Ometz Lesarev (Courage to Refuse) movement was established, I have returned again and again to Laor's texts . . .

. . . The voice is that of a poetic persona through whose life the "situation" passes and touches everything he has, grasping and refusing to let go. The child, the wife, the hours of wakefulness alone at night, memory, the very act of writing—everything is political. And from the other extreme, every terror attack, every act of occupation, every moral injustice—everything is completely personal.

. . . This is . . . a poetry that does not seek parental approval or any other approval, a poetry that liberates from the limitations of criticism of the discourse, and a poetry that . . . finds the independent place that revolts and refuses.

Did Laor's poetry "work"? Did Zonsheine's commitment "work"? In either sense of the word, at any given moment, how do we measure? If we say no, does that mean we give up on poetry? On resistance? With such obedience?

"Something I was forbidden to see."

6

Critical discourse about poetry has said little about the daily conditions of our material existence, past and present: how they imprint the life of the feelings, of involuntary human responses—how we glimpse a blur of smoke in the air, look at a pair of shoes in a shop window, at a woman asleep in her car or a group of men on a street corner, how we hear the whir of a helicopter or rain on the roof or music on the radio upstairs, how we meet or avoid the eyes of a neighbor or a stranger. That pressure bends our angle of vision whether we recognize it or not. A great many well-wrought, banal poems, like a great many essays on poetry and poetics, are written as if such pressures didn't exist. But this only reveals their existence.

It's sometimes taken that politicized emotions belong solely to the "oppressed" or "disenfranchised" or "outraged," or to a facile liberalism. Can it still be controversial to say that an apparently disengaged poetics may also speak a political language—of self-enclosed complacency, passivity, opportunism, false neutrality—or that such poetry can simply be, in Mayakovsky's phrase, a "cardboard horse"?

But when poetry lays its hand on our shoulder, as Yitzhak Laor's poem did for David Zonsheine, we are, to an almost physical degree, touched and moved. The imagination's roads open before us, giving the lie to that slammed and bolted door, that razor-wired fence, that brute dictum *"There is no alternative."*

Of course, like the consciousness behind it, behind any art, a poem can be deep or shallow, visionary or glib, prescient or stuck in an already lagging trendiness. What's pushing the grammar and syntax, the sounds, the images—is it the constriction of literalism, fundamentalism, professionalism—a stunted language? Or is it the great muscle of metaphor, drawing strength from resemblance in difference? The great muscle of the unconstricted throat?

I'd like to suggest this: If there's a line to be drawn, it's not so much between secularism and belief as between those for whom language has metaphoric density and those for whom it is merely formulaic—to be used for repression, manipulation, empty certitudes to ensure obedience.

And such a line can also be drawn between ideologically obedient hack verse and an engaged poetics that endures the weight of the unknown, the untracked, the unrealized, along with its urgencies for and against.

7

Antonio Gramsci wrote of the culture of the future that "new" individual artists can't be manufactured: art is a part of society—but that to imagine a new socialist society is to imagine a new kind of art that we can't foresee from where we now stand. "One must speak," Gramsci wrote, "of a struggle for a new culture, that is, for a new moral life that cannot but be intimately connected to a new intuition of life, until it becomes a new way of feeling and seeing reality and, therefore, a world intimately ingrained in 'possible artists' and 'possible works of art.'"

In any present society, a distinction needs to be made between the "avant-garde that always remains the same"—what a friend of mine has called "the poetry of false problems"—and a poetics searching for transformative meaning on the shoreline of what can now be thought or said. Adonis, writing of Arab poetry, reminds Arab poets that "modernity should be a creative vision, or it will be no more than a fashion. Fashion grows old from the moment it is born, while creativity is ageless. Therefore not all modernity is creativity, but creativity is eternally modern."

For now, poetry has the capacity—in its own ways and by its own means—to remind us of something we are forbidden to see. A forgotten future: a still-uncreated site whose moral architecture is founded not on ownership and dispossession, the subjection of women, torture and bribes, outcast and tribe, but on the continuous redefining of freedom—that word now held under house arrest by the rhetoric of the "free" market. This ongoing future, written off over and over, is still within view. All over the world its paths are being rediscovered and reinvented: through collective action, through many kinds of art. Its elementary condition is the recovery and redistribution of the world's resources that have been extracted from the many by the few.

There are other ghostly presences here along with Hugh

MacDiarmid: Qaifi Azami. William Blake. Bertolt Brecht. Gwendolyn Brooks. Aimé Césaire. Hart Crane. Roque Dalton. Rubén Darío. Robert Duncan. Faiz Ahmed Faiz. Forugh Farrokhzad. Robert Hayden. Nazim Hikmet. Billie Holiday. June Jordan. Federico García Lorca. Audre Lorde. Bob Marley. Vladimir Mayakovsky. Thomas McGrath. Pablo Neruda. Lorine Niedecker. Charles Olson. George Oppen. Wilfred Owen. Pier Paolo Pasolini. Dahlia Ravikovitch. Edwin Rolfe. Muriel Rukeyser. Léopold Senghor. Nina Simone. Bessie Smith. César Vallejo.

I don't speak these names, by the way, as a canon: they are voices mingling in a long conversation, a long turbulence, a great, vexed, and often maligned tradition, in poetry as in politics. The tradition of radical modernism, which crosses and recrosses the map of poetry. The tradition of those who have written against the silences of their time and location. Without it—in poetry as in politics—our world is unintelligible.

A friend asks: And what about Baudelaire, Emily Dickinson, T. S. Eliot, Gerard Manley Hopkins, D. H. Lawrence, Montale, Plath, Ezra Pound, Rilke, Rimbaud, Wallace Stevens, Yeats? In the context of that conversation, their poems flare up anew, signals flashing across contested, even infected waters. I'm not talking about literary "intertextuality" or a "world poetry" but about what Muriel Rukeyser said poetry can be: *an exchange of energy,* which, in changing consciousness, can effect *change in existing conditions.*

Translation can both betray and make possible that exchange of energy. I've relied—both today and in my lifelong sense of what poetry can be—on translation: the carrying-over, the trade routes of language and literature. And the questions of who is translated, who are the translators, how and by whom the work is done and distributed are also, in a world of imbalanced power and language, political questions. Let's bear in mind the Triangle Trade as a quintessential agony of translation.

In his *Poetics of Relation* Édouard Glissant meditates on the transmutations opening out of that abyss of the Middle Passage. He writes of the Caribbean that

> **though this experience [of the abyss] made you, original victim . . . an exception, it became something shared, and made us, the descendants, one people among others. Peoples do not live on exception. Relation is not made up of things that are foreign but of shared knowledge. . . .**
>
> **This is why we stay with poetry. . . . We know ourselves as part and as crowd, in an unknown that does not terrify. We cry our cry of poetry. Our boats are open, and we sail them for everyone.**

Finally: there is always that in poetry which will not be grasped, which cannot be described, which survives our ardent attention, our critical theories, our classrooms, our late-night arguments. There is always (I am quoting the poet/translator Américo Ferrari) "an unspeakable where, perhaps, the nucleus of the living relation between the poem and the world resides."

The living relation between the poem and the world: difficult knowledge, operating theater where the poet, committed, goes on working.

"Knowing What City You're In, Who to Talk To": LeRoi Jones's *The Dead Lecturer*

A SPLINTER OF language flares into mind before sleep, in crawling traffic or some waiting room of defunct magazines. So, a few years ago a phrase began stalking me: *A political art, let it be / tenderness* . . . words of a poem from *The Dead Lecturer* by LeRoi Jones (afterward to become Amiri Baraka). I found the book, the poem ("Short Speech to My Friends"), then pored through the pages, as after some long or lesser interval one reads poetry as if for the first time. I'd been taken, unsettled, by these poems in the late 1960s; read some of them with basic writing students at City College of New York and graduate students at Columbia. My Grove Press paperback, with the young poet's photograph on the cover, has titles and pages scribbled inside the back and front covers, faint pencil lines along margins. A traveled book, like a creased and marked-up map.

I read it again partly for the feeling of a time and place, personal and historical: New York in the late 1960s, surges of public expectation and anger, war news, assassination news,

First published in *Boston Review* vol. 34, no. 1 (March / April 2009).

political meetings, demonstrations, posters and leaflets, a time lived in the streets, in community centers, lecture halls, and student cafeterias, storefronts and walk-ups; coffeehouses, jazz clubs, living rooms, and open-air poetry readings from the East Village to the Upper West Side to Harlem. A time when factions might clash but there was motive and hope in social participation. I read it again, realizing, forty years later, how Jones's poetics had furthered my sense of possibilities when I was writing the poems of *The Will to Change* and *Diving into the Wreck*. But I return to it here for reasons beyond the personal.

Amiri Baraka's distinguished, embattled history as poet, small-press editor, essayist, playwright, political activist, autobiographer, and public figure is not what I want to write about here—even if I thought I could do it justice. Paul Vangelisti, in his foreword to *Transbluesency: The Selected Poems of Amiri Baraka/LeRoi Jones, 1961–1995* (New York: Marsilio, 1995), and Robert Creeley, in an essay (*Boston Review* [December 1996/January 1997]), provide valuable perspectives on a major poetic career. But I'd urge any serious student of the human scene, certainly any poet, who hasn't recently, or ever, read *The Dead Lecturer*: —borrow a copy from the public library, from a friend's bookshelf, or get hold of it secondhand. ("Used," "As New," "Slightly Worn," say the mail-order book catalogues. Here, both *used* and *new,* in different senses.) Many of the poems are included in *Transbluesency,* but the book itself is out of print.

And it is a book, not an assemblage of occasional poems: a soul journey borne in conflictual music, faultless phrasing. Music, phrasing of human flesh longing for touch, mind fiercely working to decipher its predicament. Titles of poems are set sometimes in bold, sometimes italics, implying structures within the larger structure. Drawing both on black music and the technical innovations of American modernism, Jones had moved deeper into a new poetics, what the poet June Jordan would name "the intimate face of universal struggle."

But intimacy is never simple, least of all in poems like these, where "inept tenderness" ("A Poem for Neutrals") searches for an ever-escaping mutuality. Or, in "Footnote to a Pretentious Book":

Who am I to love
so deeply? As against
a heavy darkness, pressed
against my eyes. Wetting
my face, a constant trembling
rain.

A long life, to you. My friend. I
tell that to myself, slowly, sucking
my lip. A silence of motives / empties
the day of meaning.
What is intimate
enough? What is
beautiful?

It is slow unto meaning for
any life. If I am an animal, there

is proof of my living. The fawns
and calves
of my age. But it is steel that falls
as a thin mist into my consciousness. As a fine
ugly spray, I have made
some futile ethic
with.

"Changed my life?" As the dead man
pacing at the edge of the sea. As
the lips, closed
for so long, at the sight
of motionless
birds.
There is no one to entrust with
meaning. (These sails go by, these small
deadly animals.)
And meaning? These words?
Were there some blue expanse
of world. Some other
flesh, resting
at the roof
of the world . . .
you could say of me,
that I was truly
simpleminded.

No lyric of romantic loneliness and melancholy here. The title suggests some literary classic presumed to have changed a life. But "It is slow unto meaning for / any life." "Who am I to love / so deeply? . . . What is intimate / enough? What is / beautiful? . . . And meaning? These words?" Images bind these questions, render them sensuous: darkness and rain, the sucked lip, the young animals, steel "that falls as a thin mist . . . a fine / ugly spray," the immobility of "the dead man pacing," "the lips, closed / for so long," the "motionless birds." Together they conjure a landscape of withholding, longing, and mistrust. The speaker is not, cannot be, "simpleminded."

In "An Agony. As Now" (possibly one of Jones's most quoted poems—at least the first few lines), contactlessness, self-barricading, are evoked but can't utter themselves; nor can "love" decipher them from the outside. But this is not simply one person's crisis. Robert Creeley rightly saw in it "life . . . in a literal body which the surrounding 'body' of the society defines as hateful"—an unacceptable condition. It can be read as common existential anguish; but to ignore that surround of social hatred is to mis-take the poem's diagnostic power:

I am inside someone
who hates me. I look
out from his eyes. Smell
what fouled tunes come in
to his breath. Love his
wretched women.

Slits in the metal, for sun. Where
my eyes sit turning, at the cool air

the glance of light, or hard flesh
rubbed against me, a woman, a man,
without shadow, or voice, or meaning.

This is the enclosure (flesh,
where innocence is a weapon. An
abstraction. Touch. (Not mine.
Or yours, if you are the soul I had
and abandoned when I was blind and had
my enemies carry me as a dead man
(if he is beautiful, or pitied.

It can be pain. (As now, as all his
flesh hurts me.) It can be that. Or
pain. As when she ran from me into
that forest.
                    (Or pain, the mind
silver spiraled whirled against the
sun, higher than even old men thought
God would be. Or pain. And the other. The
yes. (Inside his books, his fingers. They
are withered yellow flowers and were never
beautiful.) The yes. You will, lost soul, say
"beauty." Beauty, practiced, as the tree. The
slow river. A white sun in its wet sentences.

Or, the cold men in their gale. Ecstasy. Flesh
or soul. The yes. (Their robes blown. Their bowls
empty. They chant at my heels, not at yours. Flesh
or soul, as corrupt. Where the answer moves too quickly.
Where the God is a self, after all.)

Cold air blown through narrow blind eyes. Flesh,
white hot metal. Glows as the day with its sun.
It is a human love, I live inside. A bony skeleton
you recognize as words or simple feeling.

But it has no feeling. As the metal, is hot, it is not,
given to love.

It burns the thing
inside it. And that thing
screams.

"Self-hatred" is too shallow a psychologizing of such a condition.

If the poems are intimate, they are also prophetic—reaching toward drastic language to point to a constructed landscape of destruction: "love," "beauty," "God," the blind withered "yes" repeatedly countered by pain; false innocence become weapon.

Flesh, and cars, tar, dug holes beneath stone
a rude hierarchy of money, band saws cross out
music, feeling. Even speech, corrodes.
I came here
from where I sat boiling in my veins, cold fear
at the death of men, the death of learning, in
cold fear, at my own. . . .

. . . So complete, their mastery, of these
stupid niggers. Loud spics kill each other, and will not

make the simple trip to Tiffany's. Will not smash their stainless
heads, against the simpler effrontery of so callous a code as gain.

—"A contract (for the destruction and rebuilding of Paterson"

(On the back cover of my 1964 edition of *The Dead Lecturer,* the publisher quotes a then-influential New York anthologist and reviewer, describing Jones's first collection, *Preface to a Twenty-Volume Suicide Note*, in these terms: "a natural gift for quick, vivid imagery . . . spontaneous humor . . . sardonic or sensuous or slangily knowledgeable." I quote this paternalistic nonsense both to suggest what Jones, as a young black poet, was up against, and as an example of the cultural clichés into which apparently well-intentioned criticism can sink.) In his scathing and poignant "A Poem for Willie Best," Jones quotes the dominant racist "line" on "the Negro": "Lazy / Frightened / Thieving / Very potent sexually / Scars / Generally Inferior / (but natural rhythms." Such terms may have gone underground but still haunt popular imaginations via television and film—African American political and celebrity figures notwithstanding.

Here is self-wrestling of a politicized human being, an artist/intellectual, writing among the white majority avant-garde at a moment when African revolutions and black American militance seemed to be converging in the electrical field of possible liberations. Experiencing the American color line—that deceptively, murderously, ever-shifting, ever-intransigent construct—as neither "theme" nor abstraction, but as disfiguring all life, and in a time when "revolution" was still a political, not a merchandising term, Jones's poems both compress and stretch the boundaries of the case. Their geography includes the Negro character actor Willie Best, Billie Holiday (as "Crow Jane," after Yeats's "Crazy Jane" poems); the civil rights leader Robert Williams, the poets Edward Dorn (to whom the book is dedicated) and Robert Duncan (cited in two poems); Sartre, Valéry ("as Dictator"); Marx. Lyrically tough as deepest blues, they do not romanticize the black populace as some revolutionary vanguard.

> **It cannot come**
> **except you make it**
> **from materials**
> **it is not**
> **caught from. (The philosophers**
> **of need, of which**
> **I am lately**
> **one,**
> **will tell you. "The People,"**
> **(and not think themselves**
> **liable**
> **to the same**
> **trembling flesh). I say now, "The People,**
> **as some lesson repeated, now,**
> **the lights are off, to myself,**
> **as a lover, or at the cold wind.**
>
> **Let my poems be a graph**
> **of me. (And they keep**
> **to the line, where flesh**
> **drops off. You will go**

blank at the middle. A
dead man.
But
die soon, Love. If
what you have for
yourself, does not
stretch to your body's
end.
(Where, without
preface,
music trails, or your fingers
slip
from my arm

—"Balboa, the Entertainer"

In Audre Lorde's words, "the difference between poetry and rhetoric."

Out of the verse experiments of the Williams–Olson–Duncan–Creeley generation, LeRoi Jones had come into association with younger white contemporaries like Edward Dorn, Diane Wakoski, Gary Snyder, Philip Whalen, Diane di Prima, Carol Bergé. (All of these and others were published in chapbooks under Jones's editorship through his imprint, Totem Press, along with his first collection, *Preface to a Twenty-Volume Suicide Note*.)

In *The Dead Lecturer* he has taken what he needs for breath and measure, committed to the break with anglicized formalism he calls for in "The Myth of a 'Negro Literature,'" his 1962 address to the American Society for African culture:

> **No poetry has come out of England of any importance in forty years, yet there are would-be Negro poets who reject the gaudy excellence of 20th century American poetry in favor of disemboweled Academic models of second-rate English poetry. . . . It would be better if such a poet listened to Bessie Smith sing *Gimme a Pigfoot*, or listened to the tragic verse of a Billie Holiday, than to imperfectly imitate the bad poetry of the ruined minds of Europe.**

Yet the poems in *The Dead Lecturer* cannot be called derivative or said to belong to any single "school," so imprinted are they with the intensity of Jones's own personality, intellect, and location. It's the book of an artist contending, first of all with himself, his sense of emotional dead ends, the limits of poetic community, the contradictions of his assimilation by that community, his embrace and rejection of it: searching what possible listening, what possible love or solidarity might exist out beyond those contradictions. The book of a young artist doing what some few manage or dare to do: question the foundations of the neighborhood in which he or she has come of age and received affirmation. Because Jones himself is implicated, this is double-sided, and sides will be chosen.

"Short Speech to My Friends" moves to the crux of the matter. The voice at the beginning of the poem rehearses utopian desire and opposes it against actual disjuncture:

A political art, let it be
tenderness, low strings the fingers

touch, or the width of autumn
climbing wider avenues, among the virtue
and dignity of knowing what city
you're in, who to talk to, what clothes
—even what buttons—to wear. I address

/ the society
the image, of
common utopia.

/ The perversity
of separation, isolation,
after so many years of trying to enter their kingdoms,
now they suffer in tears, these others, saxophones whining
through the wooden doors of their less than gracious homes.
The poor have become our creators. The black. The
thoroughly
ignorant.

Let the combination of morality
and inhumanity
begin.

"Inhumanity": dehumanization in the eyes of others, entrenched power that inflicts suffering without compunction, and the violence (mostly horizontal) embraced by those who feel no stake in the social compact. A "political art" can't claim to imagine a "common utopia" or evoke "tenderness" while enduring this dual inhumanity. But it must somehow bear tenderness for those who "after so many years of trying to enter their kingdoms, / now . . . suffer in tears" as the poem continues. (Or, in "Balboa, the Entertainer": "But / die soon, Love. If / what you have for / yourself, does not / stretch to your body's / end.") The last three lines of "Short Speech" flash a signal toward Frantz Fanon's great study of colonialist violence, pathology, culture, and national consciousness, *The Wretched of the Earth.*

The poem's structure spirals like a staircase, where "/ the society / the image, of / common utopia" turns sharply into "/ The perversity / of separation, isolation," this turn signaled by a full-stop and capital letter. And, since the poet is located between worlds, there is a necessary ambiguity to the pronouns, the "they" and the "our."

The poem from which the book's title is taken carries his predicament to the edge:

I Substitute for the Dead Lecturer

> ***What is most precious, because***
> ***it is lost. What is lost,***
> ***because it is most***
> ***precious.***

They have turned, and say that I am dying. That
I have thrown
my life
away. They
have left me alone, where
there is no one, nothing

save who I am. Not a note
nor a word.
                    Cold air batters
the poor (and their minds
turn open
like sores). What kindness
What wealth
can I offer? Except
what is, for me,
ugliest. What is
for me, shadows, shrieking
phantoms. Except
they have need
of life. Flesh
at least,
            should be theirs.

The Lord has saved me
to do this. The Lord
has made me strong. I
am as I must have
myself. Against all
thought, all music, all
my soft loves.

                    For all these wan roads
I am pushed to follow, are
my own conceit. A simple muttering
elegance, slipped in my head
pressed on my soul, is my heart's
worth. And I am frightened

that the flame of my sickness
will burn off my face. And leave
the bones, my stewed black skull,
an empty cage of failure.

What can the practice of the middle-class avant-garde artist offer a downpressed and (formally) uneducated people who need poetry, beauty, as much as, or more than, any? who possess elaborate cultural traditions of language and music—of which Jones is well aware, if disdained by his middle-class professors at Howard University—yet from whom, in his present life, he feels ruptured? Fellow artists, unable to feel or hear Jones's shrieking phantoms, have left him alone with it all. ("They have turned, and say that I am dying. That / I have thrown / my life / away.") The voices are internal also: How to give flesh to shadows? This is the beset, conflicted art of one experiencing—allowing himself to experience—a split at the core: *Who and what do I work for? What can I offer? What city am I living in? Who am I talking to?* There is no "universal" city but that defined by those who think they rightfully own the cities.

The question has engaged many other poets, in cultures outside North America, who believed that art must be a human resource in any genuine seismic shift, that it should belong to those who need it most. But rarely in North America has there appeared so morally problematized, artistically self-critical a poetic document. Jones's fusion of craft and emotional volatility can possess a furious eloquence reminiscent at times of Aimé Césaire.

Allen Ginsberg's *Howl* broke expressive limits in 1955 beginning with the wreckage of intelligence ("I saw the best minds of my generation destroyed by madness") through the desperation beneath numbed, Freudianized, complacent postwar America. *Howl* transposed despair and alienation from individual pathology onto that society itself. In this it is one of our great public poems. But a lot of Beat-influenced poetry, catching on to the expressive open-form Whitmanic model and the un-Whitmanic machismo, minus *Howl*'s social insights, easily devolved into self-indulgence, penile narcissism, tantrum.

In *The Dead Lecturer* there is neither rant (unless strategically placed) nor self-aggrandizing neurotic angst. There are, however, many sliding screens. "Black Dada Nihilismus" I read as bitter verbal extremism, a send-up of "Dadaist" and nihilist jabber, turned against Eurocentrism. Here Sartre, "a white man" (who had strenuously opposed the French presence in North Africa) is warned "we beg him die before he is killed." The injunction to "Rape the white girls," hurls back the deadly lie of white lynching tradition; to "Rape their fathers" an expression of sheer political impotence. Masks and voice-overs are strategic to this poem.

In "the politics of rich painters" Jones mocks the discourse of an art clique he perceives as inhabited by "faggots." Gay men are made to stand in here for the capitalist art world, its class entitlement and hypocrisy. They become the target for rank homophobia, which the poet has failed to disentangle from class (and racial) rage; the language wobbles unsteadily between the two. Minus the homophobic stereotyping, this could have been a brilliant satirical poem on the posturing of rich aesthetes:

> **. . . Whose death**
> **will be Malraux's? Or the names Senghor, Price, Baldwin**
> **whispered across the same dramatic pancakes, to let each**
> **eyelash flutter**
> **at the news of their horrible deaths. It is a cheap game**
> **to patronize the dead, unless their deaths be accountable**
> **to your own understanding. Which be nothing nothing**
> **if not bank statements and serene trips to our ominous**
> **countryside. . . .**
>
> **. . . . .**
>
> **The source of their art crumbles into legitimate history.**
> **The whimpering pigment of a decadent economy. . . .**
>
> —"The politics of rich painters"

Published in 1964, *The Dead Lecturer* is not just a transitional book in a long controversial career; it's a landmark in itself. After the assassination of Malcolm X in 1965 Jones broke with his former affiliations (including his wife and daughters), moved to Harlem, then Newark; identified for a time as a Black Nationalist (then turned from Nationalism to international socialism and Third World Marxism); and became Amiri Baraka. In these readings I have wished not to biographize the poems except as Jones gives leave within them; "Let my poems be a graph / of me." Rather, I've been drawn and held by the poet as social being, trying to pierce layers of inhumanity and bad faith, including his own, with language.

For me, perhaps for others, the legacy of LeRoi Jones from this early book is to have made so personally exposed yet so wide-lens a poetry, asking questions at the crossroads of experimentalism and political upheaval, about art, community, poverty, audience, skin, self. His torquing of language is organic to the work; he doesn't assume that either self-revelation or experiments in language can suffice. The reflexive use of "jews" and "fags" as familiar, still poisonous code names for class enemies disfigures the poet's achievement, along with misogyny and its images craving the woman victim. He was writing within conditions that continue to disfigure the American, human, scene of which he was, and is a part. Even the erratics of his art continue to be instructive on that society.

And still there is this painful, visionary music:

What comes, closest, is
closest. Moving, there
is a wreck of spirit,
a heap of broken feeling. What
was only love
or in those cold rooms,
opinion. Still, it made
color. And filled me
as no one will. As, even
I cannot fill myself.

. . . And which one
is truly to rule here? And
what country is this?

—"Duncan spoke of a process"

Notes

Iraqi Poetry Today

Page 11: "(The deaths . . . brutalities from without.)" "As statistics go, at least 655,000 Iraqis have died as a result of the occupation, now in its fifth year. . . . The figure . . . came from the British medical journal *Lancet* based on a study in July last year. The number would have risen significantly after one of the bloodiest years of the occupation"; Ali al-Fadhily, "IRAQ: The Love Stories Are Gone," Inter Press Service (June 15, 2008).

Jewish Days and Nights

Page 21: "But this *is* . . . absorb us harmlessly." "Our enemies have never all at the same time persecuted us. So we have, now and then, found protection with a generous nation. But what a cruel game over the millennia, to save us a few relays on our inevitable march around the earth. —Reb Bosh"; Edmond Jabès, *The Book of Questions,* trans. Rosemarie Waldrop, 7 vols. (Middletown, Conn.: Wesleyan University Press, 1976–1984), I, p. 138.

Page 22: "Yet diaspora . . . anti-Semitism." See Melanie Kaye/Kantrowitz, *The Colors of Jews: Racial Politics and Radical Diasporism* (Bloomington: Indiana University Press, 2007).

Page 22: "Where do you come from . . . where I was born." Jabès, I, p. 139.

Page 22: "I am a Levantine . . . neighboring countries." Shulamith Hareven, *The Vocabulary of Peace: Life, Culture, and Politics in the Middle East*

(San Francisco: Mercury House, 1995), pp. 82–83, 86. For a deeper critical and historical exploration, see Ammiel Alcalay, *After Jews and Arabs: Remaking Levantine Culture* (Minneapolis: University of Minnesota Press, 1993).

Page 23: "This orthodoxy . . . official Jewish voice." "There is no elected body that is authorized to speak on behalf of American Jews. The Conference of Presidents of Major [American] Jewish Organizations, with a right-of-center orientation, has presumed to fill that vacuum, and they have consistently supported the policies of right-wing Israeli governments in the name of American Jews. The American Israeli [*sic*] Public Affairs Committee (AIPAC) exists for the purpose of lobbying Congress to support Israeli governmental policies and actions. These oligarchies have persistently reduced Israel to their ideological preferences by ignoring its critical opposition. . . . One might have hoped that religious Jews who pray several times a day for peace and who affirm the traditional teachings about the supreme worth of human life would rise up against the subjugation and humiliation of the Palestinians. Most regrettably the opposite has been the case"; Rabbi Ben-Zion Gold, "The Diaspora and the Intifada," *Boston Review* 27, no. 5 (October–November 2002).

Page 24: "Recently I was speaking . . . outside the community." Clare Kinberg, "Doing Pro-Israel Peace Work in the United States," *Nashim: A Journal of Jewish Women's Studies and Gender Issues* 6 (Fall 2003): 21–28.

Page 25: "That intellectual price . . . 'pro-Israel' allies." "The Zionist Organization of America recently [2002] presented its State of Israel Friendship Award to Pat Robertson, who has declared America to be a 'Christian nation' and believes in the conversion of the Jews after the Second Coming"; *The Nation* (January 6, 2003), p. 8.

Page 28: "As long as . . . a Middle East federation." Isaac Deutscher, *The Non-Jewish Jew and Other Essays,* ed. Tamara Deutscher (1968; repr. Boston: Alyson, 1982), pp. 116–117.

Page 30: "to discover . . . a long way." Gold, above.

Page 32: "Sometimes it is only . . . listening." Deutscher, p. 117.

Page 32: "remembering instead of thinking." Nadine Gordimer, *A Sport of Nature* (New York: Penguin, 1988), p. 234.

Page 33: "The most thoughtful . . . still a Jew?" Jabès, I, p. 61.

Page 33: "None of us . . . is chained." Solomon Burke, "None of Us Are Free," *Don't Give Up on Me*, Fat Possum Records, © 2002.

Muriel Rukeyser for the Twenty-first Century

Page 37: "The New Bridge." First published in *Vassar Review* (February 1932), uncollected; source: Kate Daniels, ed., *Poetry East* nos. 16 and 17 (1985): 34.

Page 39: "No woman poet . . . before Rukeyser." Louise Kertesz, *The Poetic Vision of Muriel Rukeyser* (Baton Rouge: Louisiana State University Press, 1980), p. 84.

Page 40: "To live as poet . . . strengthens the other." Muriel Rukeyser, "Under Forty: A Symposium on American Literature and the Younger Generation of American Jews," *Contemporary Jewish Record* 5, no. 7 (February 1944).

Page 47: "More than most poets . . . a conversation of one." Suzanne Gardinier, *A World That Will Hold All the People* (Ann Arbor: University of Michigan Press, 1996), p. 44.

The Baldwin Stamp

Page 56: "within the experience and outside of it at the same time." James Baldwin, "Sermons and Blues," review of *Selected Poems of Langston Hughes, New York Times* (March 29, 1959).

Three Classics for New Readers: Karl Marx, Rosa Luxemburg, Che Guevara

Page 58: "an association . . . for the free development of all." Karl Marx and Friedrich Engels, "The Communist Manifesto," in *Manifesto: Three*

Classic Essays on How to Change the World—Che Guevara, Rosa Luxemburg, Karl Marx and Friedrich Engels (Melbourne/New York/Havana: Ocean Press, 2005), p. 53.

Page 58: "The revolution is not . . . to orient that capacity." Che Guevara, "Speech to Medical Students and Health Workers," in *Che Guevara Reader,* 2nd ed. (Melbourne and New York: Ocean Press, 2003), p. 115.

Page 60: "I went to see . . . facing life with dignity." Che Guevara, *The Motorcycle Diaries: Notes on a Latin American Journey,* new, expanded ed. (Melbourne and New York: Ocean Press, 2003), p. 70.

Page 60: "Modern bourgeois society . . . called up by his spells." Marx and Engels, p. 35.

Page 61: "Marx . . . suddenly produces . . . it must be transformed." Che Guevara, "Notes for the Study of the Cuban Revolution," in *Che Guevara Reader,* p. 123.

Page 63: "virulent male chauvinism." Raya Dunayevskaya, *Rosa Luxemburg, Women's Liberation, and Marx's Philosophy of Revolution,* 2nd ed. (Urbana: University of Illinois Press, 1991), p. 27.

Page 63: "For Social Democracy . . . its *goal.*" Rosa Luxemburg, "Reform or Revolution," in *Manifesto,* p. 71.

Page 63: "The fate of the socialist movement . . . and democracy." *Ibid.,* p. 126.

Page 64: "Legal reform and revolution . . . independent from revolution." *Ibid.,* p. 128.

Page 64: "the July 26 Movement." The revolutionary movement led by Fidel Castro that overthrew the regime of Fulgencio Batista in Cuba (1959). Its name commemorates Fidel's July 26, 1953, attack on the Moncada army barracks.

Page 65: "The new society . . . with the past." Che Guevara, "Socialism and Man in Cuba," in *Manifesto,* p. 155.

Page 65: "Revolutions are not 'made' . . . party leaders." Peter Hudis and Kevin B. Anderson, eds., *The Rosa Luxemburg Reader* (New York: Monthly Review Press, 2004), p. 328.

Page 65: "society as a whole . . . a gigantic school." Guevara, "Socialism and Man in Cuba," p. 155.

Page 65: "The bourgeoisie cannot exist . . . melts into air." Marx and Engels, p. 33.

Page 66: "The superstructure . . . protest is combated." Guevara, "Socialism and Man in Cuba," p. 161.

Page 66: "an exaggerated dogmatism . . . sought to create." *Ibid.,* p. 162.

Page 67: "disposable time." Karl Marx, *Grundrisse: Foundations of the Critique of Political Economy,* trans. Martin Nicolaus (New York: Penguin, 1983), p. 708.

Page 67: "To fight . . . 'possible works of art.'" Antonio Gramsci, *Selections from Cultural Writings,* ed. David Forgacs and Geoffrey Nowell-Smith, trans. William Boelhower (Cambridge, Mass.: Harvard University Press, 1985), p. 151.

Page 67: "the complete *emancipation . . . human,* social object." Karl Marx, "Private Property and Communism," in *The Portable Karl Marx,* ed. Eugene Kamenka (New York: Viking, 1983), p. 151.

Page 68: "In his idiosyncratic . . . contemporary perils." In Michael Löwy, *Fire Alarm: Reading Walter Benjamin's "On the Concept of History,"* trans. Chris Turner (New York: Verso, 2005).

Page 68: "the first resource of hope [is] memory itself." Aijaz Ahmad, "Resources of Hope: A Reflection on Our Times," *Frontline* (New Delhi) 18, no. 10 (May 12–25, 2001).

Dialogue and Dissonance: *The Letters of Robert Duncan and Denise Levertov*

Page 76: "in the 'Pindar' poem." See "A Poem Beginning with a Line by Pindar," in Robert Duncan, *Selected Poems*, ed. Robert J. Bertholf (New York: New Directions, 1993), pp. 64–72.

The Voiceprints of Her Language

Page 84: "voiceprints of language." Introduction, *Soulscript: A Collection of African American Poetry,* ed. June Jordan (Garden City, N.Y.: Doubleday, 1970; repr. New York: Harlem Moon, 2004), p. xx.

Permeable Membrane

Page 98: "The presence of a problem . . . A social command." Vladimir Mayakovsky, *How Are Verses Made?,* trans. G. M. Hyde (London: Jonathan Cape, 1970), p. 18.

Page 98: "We also have to work . . . to achieve our objective." Vice President Dick Cheney, on NBC's *Meet the Press* (September 16, 2001).

Page 99: "A writer describes . . . out on the ocean." Nadine Gordimer, "The Congo River," in her *The Essential Gesture: Writing, Politics, and Places,* ed. Stephen Clingman (New York: Knopf, 1988), p. 15.

Page 99: "The poet bursts . . . the end of bonds." *Selected Poems of René Char,* ed. Mary Ann Caws and Tina Jolas (New York: New Directions, 1992), p. 125: "La poète fait éclater les liens de ce qu'il touche. Il n'enseigne pas la fin des liens."

"Candidates for My Love": Three Gay and Lesbian Poets

Page 101: "[W]hat *is* . . . social inequality." Joan Larkin and Elly Bulkin, eds., *Amazon Poetry: An Anthology* (Brooklyn, N.Y.: Out & Out Books, 1975).

Page 103: "Some of the best . . . anything at all." Essex Hemphill, *Ceremonies: Prose and Poetry* (New York: Plume, 1992), pp. 40–41.

Page 104: "We are facing . . . unpopular message?" Melvin Dixon, *Love's Instruments* (Chicago: Tia Chucha Press, 1995), p. 74.

Page 105: "That year . . . what you are." Adrienne Rich, *Dark Fields of the Republic: Poems 1991–1995* (New York: Norton, 1995), p. 66.

Page 106: "We know . . . the record." James Baldwin, "The Creative Process" (1962), in *The Price of the Ticket: Collected Nonfiction, 1948–1985* (New York: St. Martin's, 1985).

Page 107: "All before . . . Fail better." James Knowlson, *Damned to Fame: The Life of Samuel Beckett* (New York: Simon & Schuster, 1996), p. 593.

Page 107: "Whoever You Are Holding Me Now in Hand" and "'Leaves of Grass' . . . an entirety." *Walt Whitman: Complete Poetry and Collected Prose,* ed. Justin Kaplan (New York: Literary Classics of the United States, Library of America, 1982), pp. 270–271, 668–669.

Page 111: "Presidents, . . . thickets of potentialities." *Robert Duncan: A Selected Prose,* ed. Robert J. Bertholf (New York: New Directions, 1995), pp. 67, 64, 8–9.

Page 115: "A Woman Is Talking to Death." Judy Grahn, "A Woman Is Talking to Death," in *The Work of a Common Woman: The Collected Poetry of Judy Grahn, 1964–1977* (Oakland, Calif.: Diana Press, 1978).

Poetry and the Forgotten Future

Pages 123–146: Bibliography

Adonis. *An Introduction to Arab Poetics.* Trans. Catherine Cobham. Austin: University of Texas Press, 1997.

Brutus, Dennis. *Poetry and Protest: A Dennis Brutus Reader.* Ed. Lee Sustar and Aisha Karim. Chicago: Haymarket, 2006.

Cárdenas, José. "Young Immigrants Raise Voices, and Hopes." *St. Petersburg* (Florida) *Times* (May 13, 2006).

Coghlan, Thomas. "Writing Poetry Was the Balm That Kept Guantanamo Prisoners from Going Mad." *San Francisco Chronicle* (July 17, 2005).

Foot, Paul. In *International Socialist Review* no. 46 (March–April 2006).

Franklin, H. Bruce. "The American Prison and the Normalization of Torture." <http://www.historiansagainstwar.org/resources/torture/brucefranklin.html>

Glissant, Édouard. *Poetics of Relation.* Trans. Betsy Wing. Ann Arbor: University of Michigan Press, 1997.

Gramsci, Antonio. *Selections from Cultural Writings.* Ed. David Forgacs and Geoffrey Nowell-Smith. Trans. William Boelhower. Cambridge, Mass.: Harvard University Press, 1985.

Holmes, Richard. *Shelley: The Pursuit.* New ed. New York: New York Review of Books, 2003.

Lai, Him Mark, Genny Lim, and Judy Yung. *Island: Poetry and History of Chinese Immigrants on Angel Island, 1910–1940.* San Francisco: Hod Doi, 1980.

MacDiarmid, Hugh. *Collected Poems of Hugh MacDiarmid.* Ed. John C. Weston. New York: Macmillan, 1967.

Mayakovsky, Vladimir. *How Are Verses Made?* Trans. G.M. Hyde. New York: Jonathan Cape/Grossman, 1974.

Nitzan, Tal, and Rachel Tzvia Back, eds. *With an Iron Pen: Twenty Years of Hebrew Protest Poetry*. Albany: State University of New York Press, 2009.

Ritsos, Yannis. *Yannis Ritsos, Selected Poems 1938–1988*. Ed. and trans. Kimon Friar and Kostas Myrsiades. Brockport, N.Y.: BOA, 1989.

Scully, James. *Line Break: Poetry As Social Practice*. Foreword by Adrienne Rich. Willimantic, Conn.: Curbstone, 2005.

Stocking, Marion. "Books in Brief." *Beloit Poetry Journal* 56 (Summer 2006).

Vallejo, César. *Trilce*. Trans. Clayton Eshleman. Intro. by Américo Ferrari. New York: Marsilio, 1992.

White, Elizabeth. "1 in 36 U.S. Residents behind Bars: U.S. Prisons, Jails Grew by 1,000 Inmates a Week from '04 to '05." Associated Press (May 22, 2006).

Whitman, Walt. *Walt Whitman: Complete Poetry and Collected Prose*. Ed. Justin Kaplan. New York: Literary Classics of the United States, Library of America, 1982.

Zonsheine, David. "A Personal and Political Moment." *Haaretz* (November 7, 2004).

Permissions

Thomas Avena's *Dream of Order*

"Sans II" and "Three Men Walking" by Thomas Avena, from *Dream of Order*. Copyright © 1997 by Mercury House.

Iraqi Poetry Today

"Every Morning the War Gets Up from Sleep" by Fadhil al-Azzawi, translated by Salaam Yousif, from *Iraqi Poetry Today*, Modern Poetry in Translation, no. 19. Copyright © 2003 by Modern Poetry in Translation.

"What Was My Choice" by Fawzi Karim, translated by Saadi A. Simawe and Chuck Miller, from *Iraqi Poetry Today*, Modern Poetry in Translation, no. 19. Copyright © 2003 by Modern Poetry in Translation.

"The Hijrah to God" by Nazik al-Mala'ika, translated by Saleh Alyafai and Jenna Abdul, from *Iraqi Poetry Today*, Modern Poetry in Translation, no. 19. Copyright © 2003 by Modern Poetry in Translation.

"Jamilah and us" by Nazik al-Mala'ika, translated by Basima Bezirgan and Elizabeth Fernea, from *Iraqi Poetry Today*, Modern Poetry in Translation, no. 19. Copyright © 2003 by Modern Poetry in Translation.

Jewish Days and Nights

Edmond Jabès, excerpts from *The Book of Questions*, volume I. Copyright © 1976 by Rosmarie Waldrop and reprinted by permission of Wesleyan University Press.

Muriel Rukeyser for the Twenty-first Century

"The New Bridge" by Muriel Rukeyser. Reprinted by permission of International Creative Management, Inc. Copyright © 1932 by Muriel Rukeyser. From *The Collected Poems of Muriel Rukeyser*, University of Pittsburgh Press, 2005.

"Letter to the Front" by Muriel Rukeyser. Reprinted by permission of International Creative Management, Inc. Copyright © 1944 by Muriel Rukeyser. From *The Collected Poems of Muriel Rukeyser,* University of Pittsburgh Press, 2005.

Excerpt from *The Life of Poetry* by Muriel Rukeyser. Reprinted by permission of International Creative Management, Inc. Copyright © 1949 by Muriel Rukeyser.

"Girl at the Play" by Muriel Rukeyser. Reprinted by permission of International Creative Management, Inc. Copyright © 1938 by Muriel Rukeyser. From *The Collected Poems of Muriel Rukeyser,* University of Pittsburgh Press, 2005.

Dialogue and Dissonance: *The Letters of Robert Duncan and Denise Levertov*

Excerpts from *The Letters of Robert Duncan and Denise Levertov*, edited by Robert J. Bertholf and Albert Gelpi. Copyright © 2003 by Denise Levertov Literary Trust, Paul A. Lacey and Valerie Trueblood, Trustees, and The Jess Collins Trust. Used by permission.

Permeable Membrane

"To Your Heart's Content" by René Char, translated by Mary Ann Caws, from *Selected Poems*. Copyright © 1992 by Mary Ann Caws. Reprinted by permission of New Directions Publishing Corp.

"Candidates for My Love": Three Gay and Lesbian Poets

"Nowhow On" by Samuel Beckett, from *Worstward Ho*. Copyright © 1983 by Samuel Beckett. Used by permission of Grove/Atlantic, Inc. and Faber and Faber Ltd.

Excerpts from "Among My Friends Love Is a Great Sorrow" by Robert Duncan. Copyright © The Jess Collins Trust. Used by permission.

Excerpt from *A Woman Is Talking to Death.* Copyright © 1974 by Judy Grahn. Reprinted by permission of Aunt Lute Books.

Poetry and the Forgotten Future

Excerpt from "The Kind of Poetry I Want" by Hugh MacDiarmid, from *Complete Poems*, Vol. II, edited by Michael Grieve and W. R. Aitken. Copyright © 1993 by Carcanet Press Limited.

Excerpt from "The Kind of Poetry I Want" by Hugh MacDiarmid, from *Selected Poetry*. Copyright © 1992 by Michael Grieve. Reprinted by permissions of New Directions Publishing Corp.

Yannis Ritsos, excerpts from "Romiosini," translated by Kimon Friar, from *Selected Poems, 1938–1988*, edited by Kimon Friar and Kostas Myrsiades, with additional translations by Athan Anagnostopoulos. Copyright © 1988 by BOA Editions, Ltd. Reprinted by permission of BOA Editions, Ltd., <www.boaeditions.org>.

"An Old Black Woman" by Dennis Brutus, from *Poetry & Protest: A Dennis Brutus Reader*, edited by Lee Sustar and Aisha Karim. Copyright © 2006 by Dennis Brutus. Used by permission of Haymarket Books.

"The Fence" by Aharon Shabtai, from *With an Iron Pen: Hebrew Protest Poetry*, translated by Peter Cole. Copyright © 2006 by Aharon Shabtai and Peter Cole. All rights reserved.

"Searching the Land" by Rami Saari, from *With an Iron Pen: Hebrew Protest Poetry*, translated by Lisa Katz. Copyright © 2006 by Rami Saari and Lisa Katz. All rights reserved.

"Knowing What City You're In, Who to Talk To": LeRoi Jones's *The Dead Lecturer*

Excerpts from *The Dead Lecturer* by Amiri Baraka. Reprinted by permission of SLL/Sterling Lord Literistic, Inc. Copyright © by Amiri Baraka.

Index